A Pedestrian Tour
through the Islands of
Guernsey and Jersey

Map of Guernsey, 1821.

A Pedestrian Tour
through the Islands of
Guernsey and Jersey

William Gerard Walmesley

Transcribed by
Kenneth C. Renault

Phillimore

1992

Published by
PHILLIMORE & CO. LTD.,
Shopwyke Hall, Chichester, Sussex

ISBN 0 85033 837 9

Printed in Great Britain by
CHICHESTER PRESS LIMITED

Dedication

Before the following Memorial of a delightful excursion, was trans-cribed, and completed, the Writer of it performed another Trip, which it is here unnecessary to allude to, further than to say, that it brought him to the happy termination of his anxieties, & opened to him a Path, which if pursued in a right spirit, leads to true Content-ment.

His amiable Companion on this occasion, was a Lady, who if not so well fitted to accompany him o'er some of the rugged steeps of his Journey, knew well how to cheer the pathway, & soothe the cares of Life, & in one sense make it worth possessing.

To Her, as the Wife, Compa-nion, Friend, he dedicates him-self, and this, his last of pedestrian Excursions ——

Land of Sand!
Nov.r 1824

List of Illustrations

Frontispiece: Map of Guernsey, 1821

A Pedestrian Tour

Through the Islands

of

Guernsey and Jersey

With Sketches of the Vicinity

of

Plymouth and Southampton

Also

A Peep into the Isle of Wight

By the Rambler thro' the Isle
of Man English Lakes & N. Wales

Land of Sand 1821

Foreword

One is indebted to Kenneth Renault for making *A Pedestrian Tour through the Islands of Jersey and Guernsey* by William Gerard Walmesley available for publication.

Although not a major work, Walmseley's account of his holiday, laced with lively comments, adds greatly to our knowledge of the islands one hundred and seventy years ago and provides us with many fascinating snippets of information which do not appear in regular histories and more formal works.

The text is much enhanced by facsimile reproductions of the pages of the original manuscript and by the author's sketches, often of well-known places, which despite the passing of the years are still easily identifiable. That of the 'Royal George', near Perelle Bay in Guernsey, I find particularly interesting.

This is an attractive addition to the many publications on Guernsey and Jersey and, although considerably longer, is reminiscent of William Taylor Money's *Diary of a Visit to Jersey, September, 1798* published by La Société Jersiaise in its *Bulletin* for 1932. It is to be hoped that other similar diaries will make their way into print in the years to come.

RAOUL LEMPRIÈRE

Jersey
April, 1992

ix

Preface

When preparing a book such as *A Pedestrian Tour* ... for publication some unusual requirements become apparent to ensure as close an acquaintance as possible with the original manuscript.

The original is a unique and attractive example of painstaking penmanship and evocative sketches from life, set down by a man of leisure of the Georgian period who was able to travel and to observe as he wished and to record those travels in his notebook or daily diary.

The original work naturally contains minor errors and differences in the spelling of place names and in proper names of friends and acquaintances, errors which can be understood and accepted from a stranger visiting our islands for the first time and for a comparatively short period.

In addition to these acceptable errors in our place-names, the writer also exhibits an innocent schoolboy uncertainty in his spelling of certain catch words such as 'yatcht', 'symetry' 'accomodate' and others, which an indulgent reader will surely accept with a smiling understanding.

To convey something of Walmesley's personal touch no attempt has been made to correct these errors other than to insert the usual convention in the appropriate place signifying that the error is of the author and not the printer! However, in order not to disturb the narrative flow, the convention has not been inserted after every example of mis-spelling.

Likewise spaces occur in the text from time to time indicating the intention to fill in the detail later, an intention that was never fulfilled. Some sketches have suffered the loss of his titles and comments on the lower edge due to trimming for the binding of the whole. The printed captions are, nonetheless, direct transcriptions of Walmesley's text. Odd notes and comments in margins appear, serving only, with those errors and omissions, to demonstrate the spontaneity of the work and to convey to the present reader an essential aspect of his endeavours to record his feelings of the moment and to portray his immediate response to the scene before him as he sketches.

Thus, present-day readers of this very personal travel diary, particularly those of us who were blessed with a childhood in the islands, may still share with Walmesley an inner warmth of feeling for the unusual, for the differences that still make birth and residence in these islands a rather special experience.

I am indebted to my friend Raoul Lemprière for his support and for his appreciative Foreword, and I am grateful, too, to Noel Osborne of Phillimore for agreeing to publish this book and for his friendly advice on all aspects of the project as I pursued it stage by stage. Particularly am I grateful for his willing agreement to the compromise of including as wide a selection as was reasonable of the sketches and facsimile pages without which the finished book would have lacked the interest and the personal imprint of William Gerard Walmesley's hand.

Lastly, but most important of all, my sincere gratitude is due to my wife whose patient transcribing from the original and whose dedicated support throughout have brought this project to a successful conclusion for all to see and read.

K. C. R.

Introduction

The Walmesleys of Sholley and Westwood Hall, Lancashire, were a numerous and strongly Catholic family whose pedigree, as recorded in Foster's *County Families of England*, 1873, begins in 1508 with Thomas Walmesley of Sholley.

Succeeding generations saw at least seven of the women becoming nuns and several of the male line taking Holy Orders. Among the latter, the best known and most influential was Charles, O.S.B., D.D., and F.R.S. of London, Berlin and Bologna. Born in 1722, Charles was a brilliant mathematician, scientist and churchman publishing several works on all three subjects.

He also entered the Church and became a Roman Catholic Bishop. He was for 40 years the Vicar Apostolic of the Western District of England. He died at Bath in 1797 just a few years after the Catholic Relief Bill of 1791 with which he was so closely identified.

Of William Gerard Walmesley, the writer of this book born *c.*1783, very little is known. Possibly overshadowed by his illustrious great-uncle Charles, and his elder brother Charles of Westwood House and Lord of the Manor of Ince, William led a quieter life. No doubt his education under the Benedictines sharpened his intellect and cultivated a delicate sensitivity of mind. This is borne out by the Dedication at the beginning of the book, written, no doubt, to Elizabeth, née Ferrers, widow of John Gerard, who died in 1822, who was to become his wife. The tenor of this Dedication and the very precise, yet flowing writing, suggests that their marriage had taken place in 1824.

Though so little formal detail is known of the man – even the dates of birth, marriage and burial cannot be positively quoted – much of his character and temperament can be gleaned from his book. Probably in a realisation of his inborn desire to travel, the recording of his journals reflects the Grand Tour in miniature. The title page mentions 'rambles' through the Isle of Man, the English Lakes and North Wales and is dated 1821, which suggests that these travels were made during his thirties and that he 'settled down' with Elizabeth aged about forty.

This final *Pedestrian Tour* manuscript was written later, from his daily journals of the time - these are mentioned on p.38 and the last page bears the initials W.G.W. 1838.

Despite extensive enquiries into the family Archives at Record Offices, Public Libraries, the British Library and to surviving members of the family, no diaries or written records of his previous journeys have been found. It may be that this *Pedestrian Tour* was the only one so meticulously written and bound, perhaps to present to his new wife, Elizabeth, so we are indeed fortunate that it has been preserved intact and that we can now read for ourselves the candid and intimate recollections of a sophisticated visitor well qualified to express his balanced opinions and criticisms of our islands.

Among such criticisms is that of the lack of country accommodation in Jersey, the party having to walk back to St Helier each evening for a bed! Guernsey, it seems, was better served with adequate accommodation in the country parishes, Monsieur Dumaresq of the *Royal George*, Pirelle Bay, receiving special praise.

Throughout the narrative there are mentions of coastal fortifications - in the vicinity of Portsmouth, Southampton, the Isle of Wight and in Jersey and Guernsey. The knowledgeable and objective observations expressed on these structures suggest service in the Army or the Navy, perhaps towards the end of, or immediately following the French Wars. His comments on the refitting of Nelson's *Victory* in Portsmouth Dockyard support this possibility but again, no record has been found in the P.R.O. or Army Record files.

The finely drawn frontispiece map of Guernsey by Capt. Will Latham, W. G. W.'s travelling companion on the journey, and dated 1821 is another indication of a formal military mind, with the coastal defences detailed, though perhaps the term Martello Tower is a mistake. Did Guernsey really have 15 of these?

Present-day readers will be intrigued by accounts of the newly-built market in St Peter Port, the characteristics of the 'natives', the gardens of the families he had visited and, most interesting of all, an account of the Battle of Jersey. This being written only 40 years after the event, it is possibly taken verbatim from one who was actually present at the scene and watched it unfolding in the Royal Square, hour by hour. This could well be the first and only eye-witness account, and here we have it in the handwriting of William Gerard Walmesley.

The original work consists of 176 pages of fine handwriting, copperplate as we would recall the term from our schooldays. To have attempted to reproduce this in its original form would have increased the cost very considerably and have limited its availability to the general reader.

As a compromise, several pages of the original, those of particular interest, have been reproduced in facsimile and interleaved with the appropriate section of the printed pages. Similarly with the illustrations drawn by W. G. W. From the great number included in the original, several have been selected of well known places in all three islands which will be instantly recognisable despite the changes the intervening 170 years have brought.

A final attempt to date his life by inference and by reference to the Walmesley Pedigree suggests that he was born *c.*1783 (shortly after his elder brother Charles), that he married Mrs. Gerard in 1824, the date of his Dedication of the book, and that he died sometime after 1838. In spite of searching enquiries to many sources no official registration of these events has been found.

It remains to record my acknowledgements to all those official sources and to all those courteous individuals who have responded to my many requests for information on William Gerard Walmesley. Whether their replies have been positive or negative, and the scarcity of available information has made the latter the more numerous, I am grateful to them all for their courtesy and advice.

Pedigree of Walmesley,

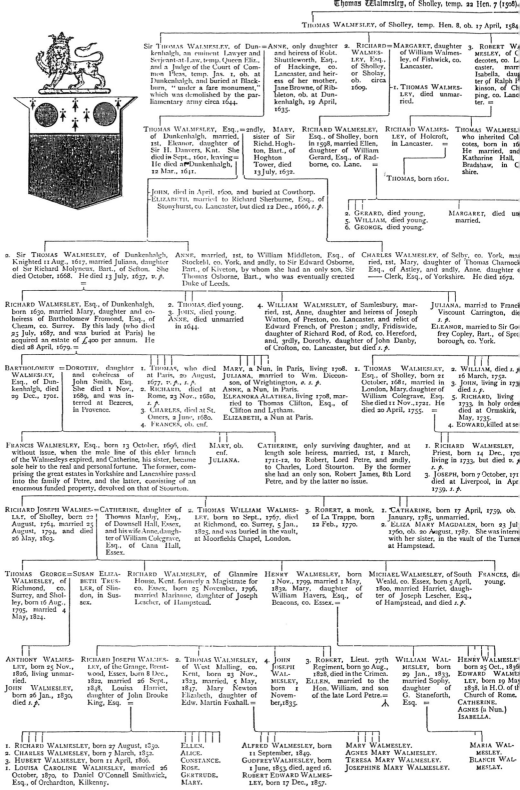

Thomas Walmesley, of Sholley, temp. 22 Hen. 7 (1508).

THOMAS WALMESLEY, of Sholley, temp. Hen. 8, ob. 17 April, 1584.

Sir THOMAS WALMESLEY, of Dunkenhalgh, an eminent Lawyer and Serjeant-at-Law, temp. Queen Eliz., and a Judge of the Court of Common Pleas, temp. Jas. 1, ob. at Dunkenhalgh, and buried at Blackburn, "under a fare monument," which was demolished by the parliamentary army circa 1644. = ANNE, only daughter and heiress of Robt. Shuttleworth, Esq., of Hackinge, co. Lancaster, and heiress of her mother, Jane Browne, of Ribbleton, ob. at Dunkenhalgh, 19 April, 1635.

2. RICHARD WALMESLEY, Esq., of Sholley, or Sholay, ob. circa 1609. = MARGARET, daughter of William Walmesley, of Fishwick, co. Lancaster.

3. ROBERT WALMESLEY, of Codecotes, co. Lancaster, married Isabella, daughter of Ralph Pilkinson, of Chipping, co. Lancaster. =

1. THOMAS WALMESLEY, died unmarried.

THOMAS WALMESLEY, Esq., of Dunkenhalgh, married, 1st, Eleanor, daughter of Sir H. Danvers, Knt. She died in Sept., 1601, leaving—He died at Dunkenhalgh, 12 Mar., 1641. = 2ndly, MARY, sister of Sir Richd. Hoghton, Bart., of Hoghton Tower, died 13 July, 1632.

RICHARD WALMESLEY, Esq., of Sholley, born in 1598, married Ellen, daughter of William Gerard, Esq., of Radborne, co. Lanc. =

RICHARD WALMESLEY, in Holcroft, in Lancaster. =

THOMAS WALMESLEY, who inherited Colcotes, born in 1606. He married, 2nd, Katharine Hall, Bradshaw, in Cheshire.

THOMAS, born 1601.

JOHN, died in April, 1600, and buried at Cowthorp.
ELIZABETH, married to Richard Sherburne, Esq., of Stonyhurst, co. Lancaster, but died 12 Dec., 1666, s. p.

2. GERARD, died young,
5. WILLIAM, died young.
6. GEORGE, died young.

MARGARET, died unmarried.

2. Sir THOMAS WALMESLEY, of Dunkenhalgh, Knighted 11 Aug., 1617, married Juliana, daughter of Sir Richard Molyneux, Bart., of Sefton. She died October, 1668. He died 13 July, 1637, v. p. =

ANNE, married, 1st, to William Middleton, Esq., of Stockeld, co. York, and 2ndly, to Sir Edward Osborne, Bart., of Kiveton, by whom she had an only son, Sir Thomas Osborne, Bart., who was eventually created Duke of Leeds.

CHARLES WALMESLEY, of Selby, co. York, married, 1st, Mary, daughter of Thomas Charnock, Esq., of Astley, and 2ndly, Anne, daughter — Clerk, Esq., of Yorkshire. He died 1672.

RICHARD WALMESLEY, Esq., of Dunkenhalgh, born 1630, married Mary, daughter and coheiress of Bartholomew Fromond, Esq., of Cheam, co. Surrey. By this lady (who died 25 July, 1687, and was buried at Paris) he acquired an estate of £400 per annum. He died 28 April, 1679. =

2. THOMAS, died young.
3. JOHN, died young.
ANNE, died unmarried in 1644.

4. WILLIAM WALMESLEY, of Samlesbury, married, 1st, Anne, daughter and heiress of Joseph Watton, of Preston, co. Lancaster, and relict of Edward French, of Preston; 2ndly, Fridiswide, daughter of Richard Rod, of Rod, co. Hereford, and, 3rdly, Dorothy, daughter of John Danby, of Crofton, co. Lancaster, but died s. p.

JULIANA, married to Francis Viscount Carrington, died s. p.
ELEANOR, married to Sir Godfrey Copley, Bart., of Sprotborough, co. York.

BARTHOLOMEW WALMESLEY, Esq., of Dunkenhalgh, died 29 Dec., 1701. = DOROTHY, daughter and coheiress of John Smith, Esq. She died 1 Nov., 1689, and was interred at Bezeres, in Provence.

1. THOMAS, who died at Paris, 20 August, 1677, v. p., s. p.
2. RICHARD, died at Rome, 23 Nov., 1680, s. p.
3. CHARLES, died at St. Omers, 2 June, 1680.
4. FRANCES, ob. enf.

MARY, a Nun, in Paris, living 1708.
JULIANA, married to Wm. Dicconson, of Wrightington, o. s. p.
ANNE, a Nun, in Paris.
ELIZABETH, a Nun at Paris.

1. THOMAS WALMESLEY, Esq., of Sholley, born 21 October, 1681, married in London, Mary, daughter of William Colegrave, Esq. She died 11 Nov., 1721. He died 20 April, 1755. =

2. WILLIAM, died s. p. 16 March, 1752.
4. JOHN, living in 1733 died s. p.
5. RICHARD, living 1733, in holy orders died at Ormskirk, May, 1735.
4. EDWARD, killed at sea.

FRANCIS WALMESLEY, Esq., born 13 October, 1696, died without issue, when the male line of this elder branch of the Walmesleys expired, and Catherine, his sister, became sole heir to the real and personal fortune. The former, comprising the great estates in Yorkshire and Lancashire passed into the family of Petre, and the latter, consisting of an enormous funded property, devolved on that of Stourton.

MARY, ob. enf.
JULIANA.

CATHERINE, only surviving daughter, and at length sole heiress, married, 1st, 1 March, 1711-12, to Robert, Lord Petre, and 2ndly, to Charles, Lord Stourton. By the former she had an only son, Robert James, 8th Lord Petre, and by the latter no issue.

1. RICHARD WALMESLEY, Priest, born 14 Dec., 1701 living in 1733, but died v. p. s. p.
3. JOSEPH, born 7 October, 1711 died at Liverpool, in Apr. 1759. s. p.

RICHARD JOSEPH WALMESLEY, of Sholley, born 22 August, 1764, married 25 August, 1794, and died 26 May, 1803. = CATHERINE, daughter of Thomas Manby, Esq., of Downsell Hall, Essex, and his wife Anne, daughter of William Colegrave, Esq., of Cann Hall, Essex.

2. THOMAS WILLIAM WALMESLEY, born 10 Sept., 1767, died at Richmond, co. Surrey, 5 Jan., 1825, and was buried in the vault, at Moorfields Chapel, London.

3. ROBERT, a monk, of La Trappe, born 12 Feb., 1770.

1. CATHARINE, born 17 April, 1759, ob. January, 1785, unmarried.
2. ELIZA MARY MAGDALEN, born 23 July 1760, ob. 20 August, 1787. She was interred with her sister, in the vault of the Turners at Hampstead.

THOMAS GEORGE WALMESLEY, of Richmond, co. Surrey, and Sholley, born 16 Aug., 1795, married 4 May, 1824. = SUSAN ELIZABETH TRUSLER, of Slindon, in Sussex.

RICHARD WALMESLEY, of Glanmire House, Kent, formerly a Magistrate for co. Essex, born 25 November, 1796, married Marianne, daughter of Joseph Lescher, of Hampstead.

HENRY WALMESLEY, born 1 Nov., 1799, married 1 May, 1832, Mary, daughter of William Havers, Esq., of Beacons, co. Essex. =

MICHAEL WALMESLEY, of South Weald, co. Essex, born 5 April, 1800, married Harriet, daughter of Joseph Lescher, Esq., of Hampstead, and died s. p.

FRANCES, died young.

ANTHONY WALMESLEY, born 25 Nov., 1826, living unmarried.
JOHN WALMESLEY, born 26 Jan., 1830, died s. p.

RICHARD JOSEPH WALMESLEY, of the Grange, Brentwood, Essex, born 8 Dec., 1822, married 26 Sept., 1848, Louisa Harriet, daughter of John Brooke King, Esq. =

2. THOMAS WALMESLEY, of West Malling, co. Kent, born 23 Nov., 1823, married, 5 May, 1847, Mary Newton Elizabeth, daughter of Edw. Martin Foxhall. =

4. JOHN JOSEPH WALMESLEY, born 1 November, 1835.

3. ROBERT, Lieut. 77th Regiment, born 30 Aug., 1828, died in the Crimea.
ELLEN, married to the Hon. William, 2nd son of the late Lord Petre. =

WILLIAM WALMESLEY, born 29 Jan., 1833, married Sophy, daughter of G. Staneforth, Esq. =

HENRY WALMESLEY, born 25 Oct., 1836.
EDWARD WALMESLEY, born 19 May, 1838, in H.O. of the Church of Rome.
CATHERINE.
AGNES (a Nun.)
ISABELLA.

1. RICHARD WALMESLEY, born 27 August, 1850.
2. CHARLES WALMESLEY, born 7 March, 1852.
3. HUBERT WALMESLEY, born 11 April, 1866.
1. LOUISA CAROLINE WALMESLEY, married 26 October, 1870, to Daniel O'Connell Smithwick, Esq., of Orchardton, Kilkenny.

ELLEN.
ALICE.
CONSTANCE.
ROSE.
GERTRUDE.
MARY.

ALFRED WALMESLEY, born 11 September, 1849.
GODFREY WALMESLEY, born 1 June, 1853, died, aged 16.
ROBERT EDWARD WALMESLEY, born 17 Dec., 1857.

MARY WALMESLEY.
AGNES MARY WALMESLEY.
TERESA MARY WALMESLEY.
JOSEPHINE MARY WALMESLEY.

MARIA WALMESLEY.
BLANCH WALMESLEY.

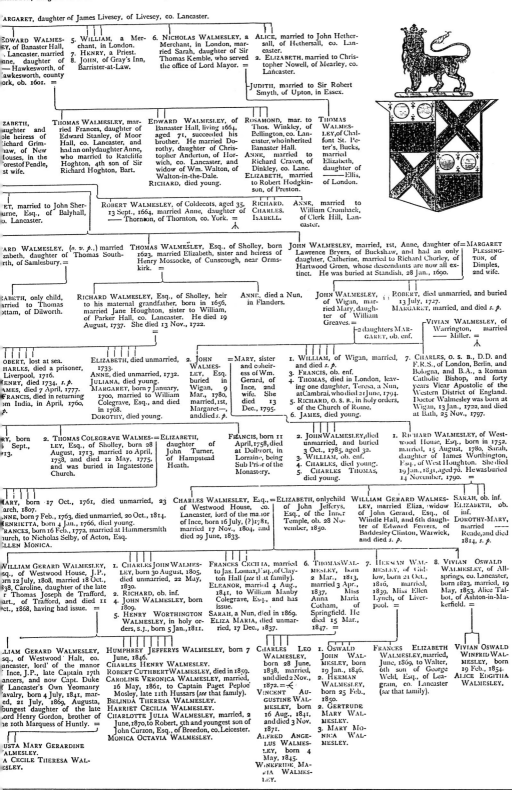

..LIZABETH, daughter of William Travers, of Neathby, co. Lancaster.

..ARGARET, daughter of James Livesey, of Livesey, co. Lancaster.

..EDWARD WALMES-
EY, of Banaster Hall,
. Lancaster, married
..nne, daughter of
— Hawkesworth, of
..awkesworth, county
..ork, ob. 1601. =

5. WILLIAM, a Merchant, in London.
7. HENRY, a Priest.
8. JOHN, of Gray's Inn, Barrister-at-Law.

6. NICHOLAS WALMESLEY, a Merchant, in London, married Sarah, daughter of Sir Thomas Kemble, who served the office of Lord Mayor. =

ALICE, married to John Hethersall, of Hethersall, co. Lancaster.
2. ELIZABETH, married to Christopher Nowell, of Mearley, co. Lancaster.

JUDITH, married to Sir Robert Smyth, of Upton, in Essex.

..ZABETH,
..aughter and
..le heiress of
..ichard Grim-
..haw, of New
..Iouses, in the
..orest of Pendle,
..st wife.

THOMAS WALMESLEY, married Frances, daughter of Edward Stanley, of Moor Hall, co. Lancaster, and had an only daughter Anne, who married to Ratcliffe Hoghton, 4th son of Sir Richard Hoghton, Bart.

EDWARD WALMESLEY, of Banaster Hall, living 1664, aged 71, succeeded his brother. He married Dorothy, daughter of Christopher Anderton, of Horwich, co. Lancaster, and widow of Wm. Walton, of Walton-in-the-Dale.
RICHARD, died young.

ROSAMOND, mar. to Thos. Winkley, of Bellington, co. Lancaster, who inherited Banaster Hall.
ANNE, married to Richard Craven, of Dinkley, co. Lanc.
ELIZABETH, married to Robert Hodgkinson, of Preston.

THOMAS WALMESLEY, of Chalfont St. Peter's, Bucks, married Elizabeth, daughter of — Ellis, of London.

..ET, married to John Sher-
..urne, Esq., of Balyhall,
..o. Lancaster.

ROBERT WALMESLEY, of Coldecots, aged 35, 13 Sept., 1664, married Anne, daughter of — Thornton, of Thornton, co. York. =

RICHARD.
CHARLES.
ISABELL.

ANNE, married to William Cromback, of Clerk Hill, Lancaster.

..ARD WALMESLEY, (o. v. p.,) married
..zabeth, daughter of Thomas South-
..rth, of Samlesbury. =

THOMAS WALMESLEY, Esq., of Sholley, born 1623, married Elizabeth, sister and heiress of Henry Mossocke, of Cunscough, near Ormskirk. =

JOHN WALMESLEY, married, 1st, Anne, daughter of Lawrence Bryers, of Buckshaw, and had an only daughter, Catherine, married to Richard Chorley, of Hartwood Green, whose descendants are now all extinct. He was buried at Standish, 28 Jan., 1690.

MARGARET PLESSINGTON, of Dimples, 2nd wife.

..ZABETH, only child,
..arried to Thomas
..ottam, of Dilworth.

RICHARD WALMESLEY, Esq., of Sholley, heir to his maternal grandfather, born in 1656, married Jane Houghton, sister to William, of Parker Hall, co. Lancaster. He died 19 August, 1737. She died 13 Nov., 1722.

ANNE, died a Nun, in Flanders.

JOHN WALMESLEY, of Wigan, married Mary, daughter of William Greaves. =

ROBERT, died unmarried, and buried 13 July, 1727.
MARGARET, married, and died s. p.

2 daughters MARGARET, ob. enf.

VIVIAN WALMESLEY, of Warrington, married — Miller. =

..OBERT, lost at sea.
..HARLES, died a prisoner, Liverpool, 1716.
..ENRY, died 1734, s. p.
..AMES, died 7 April, 1777.
..FRANCIS, died in returning from India, in April, 1760.

ELIZABETH, died unmarried, 1733.
ANNE, died unmarried, 1732.
JULIANA, died young.
MARGARET, born 7 January, 1700, married to William Colegrave, Esq., and died in 1768.
DOROTHY, died young.

2. JOHN WALMESLEY, Esq., buried in Wigan, 9 Mar., 1780, married, 1st, Margaret —, and died s. p.

MARY, sister and coheiress of Wm. Gerard, of Ince, 2nd wife. She died 13 Dec., 1795.

1. WILLIAM, of Wigan, married, and died s. p.
3. FRANCIS, ob. enf.
4. THOMAS, died in London, leaving one daughter, Teresa, a Nun, at Cambrai, who died 21 June, 1794.
5. RICHARD, O. S. B., in holy orders, of the Church of Rome.
6. JAMES, died young.

7. CHARLES, O. S. B., D.D. and F.R.S., of London, Berlin, and Bologna, and B.A., a Roman Catholic Bishop, and forty years Vicar Apostolic of the Western District of England. Doctor Walmesley was born at Wigan, 13 Jan., 1722, and died at Bath, 25 Nov., 1797.

..RY, born
..Sept.,
..13.

2. THOMAS COLEGRAVE WALMESLEY, Esq., of Sholley, born 28 August, 1713, married 10 April, 1758, and died 12 May, 1775, and was buried in Ingatestone Church.

ELIZABETH, daughter of John Turner, of Hampstead Heath.

FRANCIS, born 11 April, 1758, died at Dollwort, in Lorraine, being Sub Prior of the Monastery.

2. JOHN WALMESLEY, died unmarried, and buried 3 Oct., 1785, aged 32.
3. WILLIAM, ob. enf.
4. CHARLES, died young.
5. CHARLES THOMAS, died young.

1. RICHARD WALMESLEY, of Westwood House, Esq., born in 1752, married, 15 August, 1780, Sarah, daughter of James Worthington, Esq., of West Houghton. She died 19 Jan., 1831, aged 76. He was buried 14 November, 1790. =

..MARY, born 17 Oct., 1761, died unmarried, 23 ..arch, 1807.
..NNE, born 7 Feb., 1763, died unmarried, 20 Oct., 1814.
..ENRIETTA, born 4 Jan., 1766, died young.
..FRANCES, born 16 Feb., 1772, died married at Hammersmith ..hurch, to Nicholas Selby, of Acton, Esq.
..LLEN MONICA.

CHARLES WALMESLEY, Esq., of Westwood House, co. Lancaster, lord of the manor of Ince, born 16 July, (?) 1781, married 17 Nov., 1804, and died 29 June, 1833.

ELIZABETH, only child of John Jefferys, Esq., of the Inner Temple, ob. 28 November, 1850.

WILLIAM GERARD WALMESLEY, married Eliza, widow of John Gerard, Esq., of Windle Hall, and 6th daughter of Edward Ferrers, of Baddesley Clinton, Warwick, and died s. p.

SARAH, ob. inf.
ELIZABETH, ob. inf.
DOROTHY-MARY, married Reade, and died 1814, s. p.

..WILLIAM GERARD WALMESLEY, ..sq., of Westwood House, J.P., co. ..ancaster, lord' of the manor of ..Ince, J.P., late Captain 17th ..ancers, and now Capt. Duke ..f Lancaster's Own Yeomanry ..avalry, born 4 July, 1841, mar-..ed, 21 July, 1869, Augusta, ..oungest daughter of the late ..Lord Henry Gordon, brother of ..he 10th Marquess of Huntly. =

1. CHARLES JOHN WALMESLEY, born 30 August, 1805, died unmarried, 22 May, 1830.
2. RICHARD, ob. inf.
4. JOHN WALMESLEY, born 1809.
5. HENRY WORTHINGTON WALMESLEY, in holy orders, S.J., born 5 Jan., 1811.

FRANCES CECILIA, married to Jas. Lomax, Esq., of Clayton Hall (see that family).
ELEANOR, married 4 Aug., 1841, to William Manby Colegrave, Esq., and has issue.
SARAH, a Nun, died in 1869.
ELIZA MARIA, died unmarried, 17 Dec., 1837.

6. THOMAS WALMESLEY, born 2 Mar., 1813, married 3 Apr., 1837, Miss Anna Maria Cotham, of Springfield. He died 15 Mar., 1847.

7. HERMAN WALMESLEY, of Gidlow, born 21 Oct., 1816, married, 1839, Miss Ellen Lynch, of Liverpool. =

8. VIVIAN OSWALD WALMESLEY, of Allsprings, co. Lancaster, born 1823, married, 19 May, 1853, Alice Talbot, of Ashton-in-Makerfield. =

..LIAM GERARD WALMESLEY, ..sq., of Westwood Halt, co. ..ancaster, lord' of the manor ..f Ince, J.P., late Captain 17th ..ancers, and now Capt. Duke ..f Lancaster's Own Yeomanry ..avalry, born 4 July, 1841, mar-..ed, 21 July, 1869, Augusta, ..oungest daughter of the late ..Lord Henry Gordon, brother of ..he 10th Marquess of Huntly. =

HUMPHREY JEFFERYS WALMESLEY, born 7 June, 1846.
CHARLES HENRY WALMESLEY.
ROBERT CUTHBERT WALMESLEY, died in 1859.
CAROLINE VERONICA WALMESLEY, married, 16 May, 1861, to Captain Paget Peploe Mosley, late 11th Hussars (see that family).
BELINDA THERESA WALMESLEY.
HARRIET CECILIA WALMESLEY.
CHARLOTTE JULIA WALMESLEY, married, 2 June, 1870, to Robert, 5th and youngest son of John Curzon, Esq., of Breedon, co. Leicester.
MONICA OCTAVIA WALMESLEY.

CHARLES LEO WALMESLEY, born 28 June, 1838, and died 2 Nov., 1872. =
VINCENT AUGUSTINE WALMESLEY, born 16 Aug., 1841, and died 3 Nov. 1871.
ALFRED ANGELUS WALMESLEY, born 4 May, 1845.
WINEFRIDE MARIA WALMESLEY.

1. OSWALD JOHN WALMESLEY, born 19 Jan., 1846.
2. HERMAN WALMESLEY, born 25 Feb., 1850.
2. GERTRUDE MARY WALMESLEY.
3. MARY MONICA WALMESLEY.

FRANCES ELIZABETH WALMESLEY, married, June, 1869, to Walter, 6th son of George Weld, Esq., of Leagram, co. Lancaster (see that family).

VIVIAN OSWALD WINFRID WALMESLEY, born 19 Feb., 1854.
ALICE EDGITHA WALMESLEY.

..USTA MARY GERARDINE ..ALMESLEY.
..A CECILE THERESA WALMESLEY.

Departure from Liverpool

On Tuesday the 3.ʳ July, 1821, I & my
friend Capt.ⁿ Latham of the 1.ˢᵗ Rᵗ M.
put ourselves into the Umpire Coach for
London, designing to visit the Isle of Wight
with the islands of Guernsey & Jersey.
As the preparations for the Coronation
were going on in London with the greatest activity, we determined to give ourselves a day or two there, to view them
The whole of the public erections consisting of the covered way between the Abby
& Hall, with the Amphitheatres, from which
the procession is to be viewed, are formed
of wood, under the inspection of the Board

Departure from Liverpool

On Tuesday the 3rd July 1821 I and my friend Capt. Latham of the 1st. RLM put ourselves into the Umpire Coach for London, designing to visit the Isle of Wight with the islands of Guernsey and Jersey. As the preparations for the Coronation were going on in London with the greatest activity, we determined to give ourselves a day or two there, to view them. The whole of the public erections consisting of the covered way between the Abbey and Hall, with the, amphitheatres from which the procession is to be viewed, are formed of wood, under the inspection of the Board of Works. The angles of those streets from whence there is the slightest possibility of procuring a glimpse of the Procession, have scaffolding erected which reach to the very roofs of the buildings, and an extravagant price is demanded to secure a place. For the amphitheatre, which is intended for the Nobility and Gentry, as much as four guineas is given for a sitting.

Saturday July 7th. This morning at 8 o'clock we took our seats in the Portsmouth Coach, tired of London and its extravagance, the distance to Portsmouth is 73 miles and the fares 30/- and 18/- outside. Our route lay through Kingston, Guildford, Godalming, Liphook and Petersfield over a road the very best we had ever travelled. On reaching the summit of Portsdown, the town and Harbour of Portsmouth with all the charming scenery of the Isle of Wight and surrounding neighbourhood, burst at once on our view. A most delightful day, and high water, greatly heightened the effect. The Solent sea which divides the island from the mainland, bore on its bosom some of the proudest bulwarks of Britain, and appeared studded with innumerable vessels, which gave this prospect a claim to rank amongst the most interesting and beautiful of any. We reached Portsmouth at 5 o'clock and established our quarters at the Fountain in the High Street; we employed the remainder of the evening in viewing the Fortifications round Portsmouth and Portsea and in viewing from the Saluting Battery which is the grand lounge the packets and yatchs [*sic*], which are continually entering and departing the harbour.

Sunday 8th. We attended Divine Service at Gosport, the Rev. [ ] officiated. He is a French émigré and has a most laborious mission of it which he has fulfilled with unremitting assiduity for 23 years.

The Chapel is a very small one. Prayers commence at ½ after 9 o'clock and at 11 o'clock service is performed at the larger chapel of Portsea, to which is attached the Priest's house and at which chapel he also performs duty having no assistant. After prayers, the fineness of the day determined us to visit the fortifications of Gosport which are more complete than those of Portsmouth, tho Portsea exceeds both, being on the plan of the celebrated Vauban. They are all regular and present altogether an almost insurmountable barrier. The Blockhouse Fort is a modern work situated at the entrance of the inner harbour where the channel is only about 300 yards across. The guns are at present only mounted on the bombproof ports. Within the inner harbour are moored all the first Rates dismantled. Quitting the Blockhouse we took a view of Haslar hospital, which stands contiguous; this is a noble and extensive building, and is capable of accommodating 2000 seamen. We followed the seawall erected to protect it and which terminates and is connected with Fort Monckton; it is one mile in extent and may be about 25 feet in height. The storm & high tide of 1819 has broken it down in two places, which the workmen are at present repairing. Formerly this wall presented a straight line, but now a recess is formed in it which will allow small vessels in stress of weather to take the beach, which before at high water was impracticable. Fort Monckton is a strong but irregular work & commands effectually the anchorage at Spithead. On the land side it commands the country to Alverstoke Lake; this fort is capable of containing 600 men in bombproof casements. We proceeded along Stokes bay, the principal anchorage for Merchantmen, which is commanded by an earth work still kept up for the practice of the marine artillery; close to this work the road leads to the retired and pretty village of Alverstoke, here resided Dr. Sturgess, well known to the world for his controversy with Bishop Milner, and the house adjoining was formerly occupied by Mr. Richard Walmesley. A neat cottage displaying some beautiful strawberries at the windows tempted us to walk in and partake of them. Several bowers for the convenience of visitors were formed in the garden and we discovered from the beds of beautiful pinks that the occupier was a florist, we observed good plants of Brown's seedling, Venus Glory of Newport, dutchess of Angouleme, Hopkins No. 20 and a variety of others.

From hence we returned to Gosport passing by many neat houses and hired a boat to proceed up the harbour and give us the meeting at the Hardway, preferring the walk to that place that we might see the country and so return home by water and pay a visit to the men of war. Amongst them all first ranked the Nelson, a new ship, recently launched, and the largest in our navy, being pierced for 130 guns; we inspected her throughout, and admired the great order and neatness in which her spars, blocks and other tackle was arranged. They were stowed on the middle deck, in such a manner that the air had a free circulation amongst them; temporary stauncheons were placed under each beam; everything was on a gigantic scale. The trussel trees for the main top we had the curiosity to measure and found them to be 24 feet in length, the cap for the main topmast was formed of two solid blocks of wood firmly secured by hoops and bolts. She had everything on board with the exception of her guns and stores and might be completely equipped for sea in the course of ten days.

From the quarter deck of this ship, we viewed the Royal George yatcht [sic], then ready for the reception of his Majesty: She is about 350 tons burthen, but amongst these colossal battering engines she assumes but a pigmy form tho splendid and beautiful. We then descended to our boat and passed close along-side of her. She is pierced for 20 guns, the beadings or wreaths round the port-holes are well carved and richly guilded and the portholes are filled up with squares of plate glass; her quarter galleries present a similar appearance. We next passed close to the Victory, the late Lord Nelson's ship, she is altogether from the repairs she has undergone, a new ship; always admired for her symetry [sic] and her qualities of fast sailing, and being a good seaboat. A cross is carved on the quarter deck where Lord Nelson received his mortal wound. There are three Guard ships in commission here, the Boyne, Queen Charlotte and the York, the second is considered a handsome vessel and a good sea boat, tho the Nelson in point of beauty and size surpasses all. Not less than 40 Sail of Men of War are securely laid up in this harbour. It is capacious enough to contain three times this number in perfect security. We returned to the Fountain at 5 o'clock and after having refreshed ourselves with a good dinner and wine, which we can recommend to any of our friends, we set out again to explore the works of Southsea Castle and Fort Cumberland. The former was built during the reign of Henry the 8th and has lately undergone a complete repair; it is furnished with bombproof casements capable of containing 200 men, and effectually commands the channel on the east side of Spithead. Fort Cumberland is a regular work in the form of a pentagon, and is admired by all who see it, as a perfect model of a fortified work. It is furnished with bombproof casements capable of containing 5000 men, and commands the entrance into Langstone harbour; it also forms the Eastern defence of Hilsea island; between this work and Southsea Castle, a distance of two miles, are situated Lumps and Eastney forts; they are all now, during a state of peace, almost dismantled. We returned to the Fountain about 10 o'clock and shortly after retired to bed.

Monday 9th. This day was fixed on for our departure from Portsmouth, but as the Packet for the Isle of Wight did not sail till 3 o'clock we devoted the morning to the Dockyard. We were admitted on inserting our names in a book, and escorted by a guide, who accompanied us thro the different departments of this great naval emporeum [sic], the mast houses, Block house or manufactory and anchor smithy, chiefly attracted our notice; the latter truly reminded us of Vulcan's Forge; the bellows are singularly constructed, and blow with more than mortal force: they are composed of two immense casks, which acquire a circular motion by means of a wince [sic], worked by two of the Imps. A steam engine of

54 horse power sets in motion machinery by which the most massive bars of iron are welded together and drawn like wire to any size and to suit any purpose required, but chiefly for the making of anchors. When the mouths of the furnaces were opened, the strong vivid glare of light and the busy scene before us made us picture to our imaginations, that we were in the very place where Vulcan forged the bolts of Jove; but ere long we were reminded of their being pure mortals, made of clay which required occasional moistening, one of them stepped up to us and made his customary demand of allowance. Along the walls of the cable house were arranged anchors of all sizes, the largest we observed weighed 94 cwt 3.14. The principal store consists of a centre and two very extensive wings; it is a very magnificent building and is at present completely filled with all the materials requisite for the outfit of men of war; in cables, cordage, sails etc. We observed five ships of the first class building and repairing, they were under sheds, constructed to protect them from the weather, the roofs of some of these sheds were slated, and others coppered, pierced with many lights, they are in themselves works of wonderful labour ingenuity and expence [*sic*]. The guide receives any compensation you may choose to make him, and we retired highly gratified. Close to the common Hard, we observed an immense number of spars, secured together by piles driven into the ground, and kept there afloat at high water to preserve them from the effects of the weather; these are intended for the use of the Royal Dock yard, and occupy a very considerable space, the ground is mud and thus at low water they are still preserved from the effect of a burning sun.

We returned to the inn and had just time to make ready for the sailing of the Ryde Packet, on coming down to the Point, to embark, we observed several packets under sail, waiting to receive their passengers.

We embarked at 3 o'clock pm and in company with several other vessels, stood away under Blockhouse fort, with a fresh breeze from the westward. At half past 3 o'clock it blew very fresh and we took a reef in the mainsail. When abreast of Fort Monkton, not observing the Union at the signal staff to be half mast, we had nearly got into the line of the guns, which the marine artillery were practising from the forts on Stokes bay. A shot struck the water about 100 yards ahead of us. This however was the last shot in the locker and closed the practice of the day, for we observed the Union to be again run up, which is the signal for a cessation of firing. After a quick passage of one hour we landed at the pierhead of Ryde, a distance of 7 miles. This pier is built on piles and extends upwards of 500 yards, into the sea. We ascended the town, which is built on a steep declivity, in search of quarters and were recommended to try Lock's hotel, as being best adapted to the economy of pedestrian tourists. Here we met with civility and very comfortable accomodations [*sic*] with moderate charges. There are many pretty cottages, and marine villas peculiar to this delightful station, and we rambled about its interesting environs, admiring numerous situations, in which we could have gladly taken up our future abode, and nightfall had come on, before we could retrace our footsteps to the inn, a comfortable cup of tea and some very fine prawns left us nothing more to wish for, but a resting place for the night to prepare us for encountering the fatigues of a succeeding day.

Tuesday 10th. This morning at 7 o'clock we set out from Ryde, the road leads in a serpentine form thro the grounds of Mr. Simeon, which are covered with well grown timber. Four miles from Ryde is situated the village of Brading at the upper end of the harbour of that name which is large enough to afford shelter to fishing boats of from 20 to 30 tons. The entrance is very narrow. Here we breakfasted and afterwards looked thro the church, which has nothing to recommend it to the notice of the traveller, there are two figures carved in wood in the chancel of the Oglander family, whose mansion (Nunwell) is close adjoining. We continued our route across the country, skirting Sandown level which is a valley connecting Brading harbour and Sandown fort, thro which the sea may formerly have flowed.

The bay of Sandown is in the form of a noble crescent extending 5 miles from Culver Cliff to Dunnose point, the only convenient spot for the landing of an enemy, is under the guns of the fort, the shore for the most part being bounded by inacessible [*sic*] cliffs which are chiefly of marl or chalk.

We quitted the main road here and followed the footpath close along the margin of the cliff, which is very precipitous, and in some parts 300 feet in perpendicular height above the level of the shore.

We observed in two places landslips of very recent occurrence, which had carried away the footpath and spread over a considerable space on the shore below. The tide had not yet washed over it, the country to the right was under high cultivation and the farms scattered amongst the woods, with the heights before us, which were also partially clothed, imparted a rich variety to the scene around us. Here we observed the wild convolvulus, with many other flowers, common in our gardens, and privet was to be seen in every hedge. In the course of our walk we were surprised to see the ground cultivated to the very brink of these giddy heights. The second landslip we arrived at, carried away several yards of the growing corn, some of which we could discern still growing amidst ye ruins below. Soon after leaving Sandown Fort, we approached the situation where the Infantry barracks formerly stood, they are now levelled, but the Artillery barracks yet remain and are a fine pile of building converted now into lodgings. On the road side before we arrived at these barracks, stand two or three pretty marine cottages, overlooking the bay, one of these formerly belonged to the notorious Liberty Wilkes, but it has changed its appearance

1.   The view from the windows of the Vine Hotel, Cowes, Mr. Nash's seat opposite.

with its owners for the worse. It was used by Genl. Drummond as his head quarters, when he had the command of the brigade, consisting of 4000 men stationed on this bay in the year 1804. Two miles further on is Shanklin Chine, a deep gap penetrating half a mile inland. There are several cottages hanging on its declivities, and two or three handsome houses close to it. It forms one of the attractions to the Felicity hunters who are always to be seen during the season lounging about its picturesque environs. We passed the church belonging to this small village, near to which is a very substantial handsome farm house belonging to Mr. Hill occupied by farmer Joliffe, who has been the tenant for 30 or 40 years. The land appears rich and prettily diversified and the house commands a charming view of the sea.

Here the road took a steep ascent and from the height, we had a fine and extended view of the British Channel on the south side of the island, covered with many vessels.

Descending we passed Luccomb Chine on our left and here commences that part of the country known by the name of the Undercliff, it is a portion of undulating ground, overhung by the Downs, from which it appears to have slipped, or to have been rent, by some extraordinary convulsion, a face of fretted rock for the extent of seven miles, covered occasionally with the ivy and other creeping plants gives the idea that at some period the undercliff has formed a junction with it. From the grotesque and fanciful forms, these rocks assume, one might in part fancy they were ramparts with their flanking turrets. The land underneath seems to have rushed forward towards the sea, and has assumed the most varied form of hill and valley.

This tract is highly cultivated and harbours many sweet retreats, which are often hidden from the eye, till they present themselves in all their beauty to the delighted spectator and the taste and opulence of its several owners have distinguished and rendered this little spot the admiration of all who visit it. We noticed a part of the cliff that has seperated [*sic*] from the height above, and had covered the ground with vast fragments of rock, extending to the roadside, sweeping away trees, and surmounting every other obstacle that opposed its passage. There are several fishing coves on this side of the island, where shell fish are caught in plenty, and Lord Dysart, the Honble. Mr. Pelham, and many other gentlemen have villas on its wooded eminences.

2. Gateway of Carisbrook Castle.

A new hotel bearing the name of the Spring Rock, from a chalybeate water which is found there, terminates the road along the Undercliff, and we made a sudden bend to the right in the direction of Newport, which was distant eight miles. The small village of Niton received us at 4 o'clock, after a walk of 20 miles: at its inn we found comfortable accomodation and sat down to a good dinner; the draught porter and port wine were excellent and the beds clean and comfortable.

Wednesday 11th. A cloudless sky and serene atmosphere invited us to pursue our route at 6 o'clock this morning; we passed over an open country for four miles until the summit of Blackdown presented us with a view of the Medina vale, thro' which the river of that name flows. The country is chiefly under corn and the slopes of the vale are richly wooded. We stopped for breakfast at the only house which offers itself on the road. It is situated near the entrance of the vale, and is half way from Niton to the Capital. Though humble in its appearance it afforded the grand requisite excellent bread, which indeed we have never known the want of since we quitted London.

About 10 o'clock we entered Newport, a good well built and spacious town, situated on the banks of the small river Medina. It has an elegant Town Hall,

3. Undercliffe nr. Mirables, I. Wight.

extensive Brewery and possesses many advantages from the river being navigable up to it for flats and small craft. Several florists have their gardens in its neighbourhood and an annual show of flowers is held here and premiums awarded to the best. We visited Lock's garden to see his pinks, which we heard at Alverstoke he cultivated with great attention and success, he had an extremely fine show of these flowers, and also Sweet Williams of a rich scarlet tending to black in the centre. He frequents the Portsmouth and Southampton Prise meetings, where he has been frequently a successful candidate, we gave an order for an assortment of the pinks to be sent into Lancashire. We next visited Carisbrooke castle, ye ruins of which including the walls, are very extensive, the situation commands a fine view, and below, the beautiful little village of Carisbrooke appears, distant one mile from Newport. The outworks are more modern than the Castle itself, having been added during the reign of Elizabeth; the lines afford a most delightful promenade and the woods which have been planted close up to them renders the coup d'oeil more enchanting. It is much resorted to by the inhabitants of Newport. Lord Bolton has his residence within the walls, he is at present Governor of the island, and strangers are kindly permitted to see the lions within. The window from which King Charles is said to have made his escape is still pointed out, but is not visible from the exterior, the shrubs and trees having grown above it. After making a sketch of the Gateway of this celebrated castle, we continued our route on to Cowes, passing the extensive and well planned barracks on Parkhurst forest, which is the only Depot at present for our regular Infantry. The road ascends for a considerable distance until at length the Solent, with all its bewitching scenery opens to the view.

The Medina on our right now assumed the consequence of a river, whitened with the sails of vessels, and its banks enriched with cultivation and spangled with the villas and seats of the Nobility and gentry. Amongst all stands conspicuous, the elegant modern castellated mansion of Mr. Nash, on the right bank of the river, rearing its towers of chastest colour from amidst the rich foliage of a surrounding wood. Underneath appeared the village of East Cowes, and a winding road through woods and cultivated ground, embellished with tasteful cottages, conducted us into the opposite town of West Cowes.

This is a charming situation commanding most beautiful and animating views of the Solent sea, Southampton water and the Medina; it is very much frequented by the Yatcht Club as a sailing station. The river and roads were very much crowded with pleasure vessels and shipping, amongst which we noticed Lord Craven's ship yatch Louisa, Lord Grantham's ....., The Marquis of Anglesea's new cutter Pearl, and the Honble Mr. Pelham's brig Falcon with many others. Here are many beautiful marine cottages and villas. Lord Seymour's mansion appears amongst the woods above old Castle point adjoining Mr. Nash's. We took up our quarters at the Vine where we were comfortably accomodated our window looked upon the river which flowed up to the walls of the house and gave it the appearance of a view from the cabin windows of a ship. Vessels were constantly sailing in and out. Two steam Packets belong to this place which sail regularly twice a day to and from Southampton and Portsmouth. After a good dinner and a glass of superlative, we retired almost with reluctance to our couches.

Thursday 12th. This day at 12 o'clock we embarked on board the Steam packet for Southampton and once more crossed the Solent. The distance from Cowes to the entrance of Southampton water is ... miles and to the town of Southampton it is ... more. It is a delightful sail and on every side the eye is gratified with the most delightful scenery. The peaceful Solent bears you smoothly on, seldom causing those troublesome qualms so destructive of pleasure on aquatic excursions.

The entrance of Southampton water is commanded by Calshot Castle a stronge circular tower with a platform for guns. Vessels in sailing up keep pretty close under it, where they find deep water. The river is buoyed out up to the town, rendered necessary from the extensive mud flats on its S.W. side, which

4.   Road and entrance of the Medina, Cowes.

uncover at half ebb and confine the stream to a deep channel. The banks on both sides are sweetly wooded and the seats of several gentlemen display the happiest effect of art combined with superior natural advantages. About midway up and not far from the waters edge appears the venerable ruin of Netley Abbey and fort, forming a distinct feature in the landscape and inspiring a very different train of thoughts calculated perhaps to show the vanity of those which the moment before had occupied our whole attention. Indeed the splendour of the scene, influenced by a brilliant sun was sufficient to captivate the mind and to prevent the intrusion of any idea of a perishable nature. Vessels of all descriptions were passing by us, amongst which were many pleasure yatchts. The Causand rig has been lately introduced amongst them which substitutes a mizen in lieu of a boom, making the boat much easier at sea, but quite at variance with the smart rakish appearance so peculiar to the class of cutters. We observed one boat of the Virginian pilot boat construction and perhaps 60 tons Register, she had two taut masts raking considerably aft, the sails had a good deal of hoist and were cut very narrow in the head.

We landed at Southampton Pier, at 3 o'clock and proceeded to the Vine inn where we expected to find the portmanteau we had forwarded from Portsmouth on quitting that place on the 9th inst; we found it in safe custody of Mrs. [...] who gave us a civil reception, and as the house appeared a tolerable average of its kind, we established ourselves in it. After dinner we made enquiries about the sailing of the packets & Jersey and found they were dispatched twice a week on Wednesday and Saturday, we accordingly secured berths for Saturday. The fare in the cabin was 21/-. We could not help remarking the miserable state of the only pier at Southampton which is too small even for the various packets that frequent it. The whole place indeed on the edge of the water appears more like a decayed than a well frequented opulent sea port. We retired to our inn and very soon after to bed.

Friday 13th. A charming morning gave an additional zest to the thoughts of the little excursion we had planned for this day, and we dispatched our morning's meal with all the haste that cook and tadpoles would allow us and immediately after set out for Netley Crossing the deep narrow stream of the Hitchin [*sic*], which joins Southampton water close to the town. We took the field path leading through the grounds of [...] and on entering a wooded dingle, we found ourselves suddenly in the pleasure grounds. On advancing the woods (chiefly oak) assumed the character of the wildest forest scenery and conducted us presently to a gentle rising ground of the most beautiful verdure, at the foot of which was seen the venerable and elegant pile of Netley. A more retired appropriate spot can scarcely be conceived or wanted to give effect to a highly picturesque ruin. Surrounded by trees whose dark hues formed an agreeable contrast with the lively verdure of the ground rising on every side, but in the direction of the shore, it seemed a spot peculiarly adapted for prayer and contemplation. We passed several hours within its walls employed in endeavouring to sketch some of its beauties, during which time it attracted many other visitors; some of the females had provided themselves with the necessary implements for tracing its graceful outlines, which we observed they were very quick in accomplishing. The work of hours with us, scarcely employing them as many minutes. The Abbey and Fort were carried off before we could possess ourselves of the East or West window. The Fort is a massive piece of masonry, and stands yet entire, having presented no object for plunder, or given offence to the blind zeal of misguided fanatics.

On quitting the fort, we pursued our course along the banks of the river, which are at half ebb, flat and muddy, with some rocks. The seaweed is carefully collected and piled in heaps for the purposes we supposed of manure. At the small village of [...] where the river Hitchin joins Southampton water we ascended the road leading over [...] where a good view is obtained of Southampton, the river and opposite banks; several gentlemen's seats are seen on this eminence. We now bent our steps towards the town and descending the hill approached the stone bridge thrown over the Hitchin on the London road. This bridge takes a toll of [...] from every footpassenger: it has one principal arch, the stream at low water passing through it only, a deep bed of mud is formed under the other covered at high water. Though the river is so narrow yet it affords depth of water sufficient to admit vessels of 200 tons close to the bridge.

There are two or three yards on this stream for building vessels. After dinner we viewed the town of Southampton which consists of one principal street called the high street, well built and supplied with good shops. On ye south side of this street is an artificial mound of earth on which formerly stood the Castle. The walls were rising from their ruins some short time ago, but Lord [...] to whom it belongs is now again taking them down.

Saturday 14th. A fine calm morning. The packet was not to sail til one o'clock. The intermediate time was filled up in exploring the wall and precincts of the town. We observed near the S.E. gate leading from the beach, a very large piece of brass ordnance. The walls of the town are high on the river side on which side only they are kept up. The whole of the outskirts have a miserable neglected appearance. We provided ourselves with a few necessaries for our voyage and discharging our bill at the Vine, we repaired on board the Speedy packet Captn. Lidstone, and with a fair tho light wind, stood down the river; it suddenly however shifted to the S.W. and blew a fresh breeze. At 7 o'clock we came to an anchor outside as the flood tide and wind set strong against us.

We had now an opportunity of reviewing our companions who had embarked with us. They were enticed on deck by the quiet state of the vessel. Five of them were females, one very young and rather handsome whom we were surprised to hear had been twice married. We observed two of the party of respectable appearance still enjoying the good things they had brought on board with them and descanting on the most approved modes of dressing turtle, venison etc, one had resided in France and was going there again. We judged from appearances and from the remarks they both occasionally made, that a very slight change in the then placid state·of the elements would make a very considerable one in the aconomy of their stomachs.

We had a Lieutenant of the Navy amongst our number and an artist of some merit as a painter both natives of Guernsey, in all about 20 passengers. At 12 pm we were again under weigh, but the sea had encreased [*sic*] with the wind and the next morning the deck presented a very different scene. The Lieutenant, ourselves, and one or two more held indisputed possession of ye deck except when Alderman Turtle claimed a passage to the gangway, where he became for some time stationary with his head over the side, haranguing perhaps the fish from the noise he made, but his words were unintelligible to us.

5.   Port St. Peter & Castle Cornet from near Belgrave Battery North.

It was a lowering, damp, unpleasant day and the wind still very strong from the S.W. At 12 M. we had a sight of Alderney and Cape La Hague. We caught a mackerel with our lines and two other small fish, which the Lt. soon put into eating order; his appetite proved stronger than ours at dinner time, and we suffered him to claim the largest share without consulting the watch below, who were all employed to the best advantage.

Alderman Turtle was again seen creeping up the companion stairs, with a face of all hues, and took his accustomed station at the gangway. All was quiet below, save certain convulsive sounds, answered by pitiable sighs, until we entered the passage called the Swinge, formed by a rocky island lying on the south side of Alderney. The water was here perfectly smooth, but the tide ran against us with great rapidity and tho. we had a strong and favorable breeze we could make no headway, but remained for 2 or 3 hours as if we were at anchor, sometimes gaining a few feet and then drifting again. Twelve or fourteen chasse marees passed by, bound along the French coast. On clearing the passage at 9 pm the Casket [*sic*] lights showed on our starboard hand: they are easily distinguished from all other lights from [...] At 10 pm we turned into our berths, from whence we were roused at 5 am by a host of tadpoles who had boarded us in the dock, and who stuck their cards thro the curtains of our bed places. The cabin was all noise and confusion and we ascended the companion stairs to breathe a purer atmosphere; we soon got ourselves and luggage into a boat alongside and following the track of a tadpole we entered the [...] Inn at Port St. Peter.

Monday July 16th. At 7 oclock we cleaned and refreshed ourselves by bathing which we considered was highly necessary after being confined 41 hours on board a packet. The Speedy was admirably adapted for sailing and was a good seaboat but the essential requisite cleanliness was neglected. Capt. Lidstone had formerly sailed in her as mate, under his brother who having procured a situation in the East India company's service, left him master of her. We experienced great civility and attention from the Captain and his crew, they were extremely communicative but there appeared to be no distinction amongst them, to this want of authority and control over the men we attributed the failing complained of.

It was a lovely summer's morning, all was still and the silvery surface of the dark blue sea was broken only by the rocks, which here and there interrupted its current. After breakfast and a plentiful supply of good cream and butter peculiar to this island, we strolled out to view the town: our excursions for this day were confined to the immediate environs. We visited Fort George, Vale Castle, St. Sampson's church and harbour from which places we obtained good views of the coast scenery on this side the island.

still, & the silvery surface of the dark blue sea, was broken only by the rocks, which here & there interrupted its current. After breakfast & a plentiful supply of good cream & butter peculiar to this island, we strolled out to view the town: our excursions for this day were confined to the immediate environs. We visited Fort George, Vale Castle, St Sampson's church & harbour, from which places we obtained good views of the coast scenery, on this side the island.

Port St Peter is situated on a rapid slope; the ground on the right forming the lines of Fort George, tower above & shut it out from the south: the land on the north side is also high, but is covered with buildings & plantations, which with the gardens in & about the town, give to it an effect extremely picturesque and pleasing. The streets in the lower part of the town are after the French style, very narrow, & the houses generally three stories & oftentimes four, which creates a gloomy, & sombre appearance. There are many good shops in this part, & everything that can be wished for may be purchased at moderate prices. The higher streets forming the modern part of the town are capacious & airy, commanding beautiful prospects of the sea, with the adjacent islands of Alderney, Great and little Sark, Herm, Jettou, & Jersey. The approach to St Pierre by Vessels from the northward is generally through the channel formed by Great Sark & Jettou, called the great Russel; that lying between Herm & the island of Guernsey, is the lesser Russel. The tides set thro' these passages with the greatest rapidity, & tho' they are bouyed & marked out, they cannot be attempted with any safety by

Port St. Peter is situated on a rapid slope, the ground on the right forming the lines of Fort George, tower above and shut it out from the south. The land on the north side is also high, but is covered with buildings and plantations, which with the gardens in and about the town give to it an effect extremely picturesque and pleasing. The streets in the lower part of the town are after the French style, very narrow, and the houses generally three stories and often times four which creates a gloomy and somber appearance. There are many good shops in this part and everything that can be wished for may be purchased at moderate prices. The higher streets, forming the modern part of the town are capacious and airy commanding beautiful prospects of the sea, with the adjacent islands of Alderney, Great and Little Sark, Herm, Jettou [*sic*] and Jersey. The approach to St. Pierre by vessels from the northward is generally through the channel formed by Great Sark and Jettou called the great Russel; that lying between Herm and the island of Guernsey, is the lesser Russel. The tides set thro these passages with the greatest rapidity and tho they are bouyed and marked out, they cannot be attempted with any safety by large vessels, owing to the numerous hidden rocks. The approach from the eastward is easier. Castle Cornet stands immediately opposite the harbour, distant scarcely half a mile, it is built on a rock of granite, and is a work of considerable strength, completely

6. Cornet Castle with Le Vale Castle in distance from nr. Clarence Battery, St. George.

commanding the whole anchorage and approaches, it may sometimes be reached from the town on foot at very high spring tides. It forms an interesting feature from the harbour when shipping and men of war anchor under it. Guernsey commands a good trade to Newfoundland and the West Indies, and has many fine ships belonging to it.

An oyster fishery has lately been established by subscription, to supply the island and the London market; the fish are brought from the opposite coast of France and are deposited in beds prepared to receive them at St. Sampson's harbour. The States are giving great encouragement to this fishery, which promises to be very successful. Port St. Pierre possesses a tolerable market for fruit and vegetables and the potatoes are as good as those of Lancashire, bread is of excellent quality and cheap, being 1¾ and 2d. per lb. It can boast of a theatre, an elegant ballroom, public Baths, warm and cold, and a large building adapted for a butchers market is now erecting. There is also a handsome convenient building lately erected near the pier head as a slaughter house, the roof is of cast iron, and all the conveniences within, ladders, etc. are made of wrought iron; The tide flows close to the door and carries away the offal etc. and this place is kept extremely sweet and clean.

Tuesday 17th. This day we set out on our tour round the island. The weather was truly summer, not a cloud being visible on the horizon. We proceeded to the southward by the heights of Fort George, which command most extensive and picturesque views of the surrounding scenery and the distant shores of France. These works are very extensive and the most complete and regular of any in the island. On this road are seen several beautiful places of residence. On St. Martin's point about one mile distant from St. Pierre is a handsome column erected in honor [sic] of General Doyle, who formerly commanded in this island. It is of the Doric order 70 feet in height with a platform and iron railings, surmounted by a plain Cupola, a winding staircase leads to the summit. Near to it is one of the many signal stations, erected on the command points of the island, now abandoned. The barracks close by are occupied by three or four soldiers to preserve them from damage. This is said to be the site of a Roman work and the appearance of the ground would lead to that supposition. From this point we pursued an irregular route taking the coast in its various windings and avoiding ye beaten tracks; this proved a most laborious undertaking as the coast is indented with many bays and creeks, and is in every part extremely precipitous and rocky particularly on the southern side. Its numerous inlets afford protection to small boats in their occupations of fishing; it abounds with shell fish. It is from nature almost inaccessible to an enemy and the line of works erected in communication along its shores preclude the possibility of a landing. The bay of Petit Bo, exhibits a dark and gloomy cavern on its eastern side, and at this point after making a sketch of No. 13 Martello Tower we ascended the

St Sampson's harbour. The States are giving great encouragement to this Fishery, which promises to be very successful. Port St Pierre possesses a tolerable market for fruit & vegetables, & the potatoes are as good as those of Lancashire. Bread is of excellent quality, & cheap, being 1¾c 2° ℔; it can boast of a theatre, an elegant ball room, public Baths, warm & cold, & a large building adapted for a butchers market is now erecting; there is also a handsome convenient building lately erected near the Pier head, as a slaughter house, the roof is of cast iron, & all the Conveniences within, ladders, &c are made of wrought iron; the tide flows close to the door, & carries away the offall &c, & this place is kept extremely sweet & clean. Tuesday 17th This day we set out on our tour round the island, the weather was truly gloomy cavern on its eastern side, & at this point after making a sketch of No. 13 Martello Tower, we ascended the deep & beautiful glen leading to the village of La Forest, which is sweetly situated. From hence we pursued the coast road leading to the church of Torteval over an elevated but level & richly cultivated part of the island, yielding luxuriant crops. We obtained frequent glimpses of the sea line, & French coast. The village of Torteval is small, & straggling, but it has a handsome new church just completed, with an elegant light tower & spire. After making a sketch of it, we entered a deep road overhung by trees on either side, which conducted us to the shore of Roquaine bay, remarkable for its castle. It was low water, & the rocks, with which this part of the coast is girted, presented a most wild & grotesque

7. Headland above Fermain Bay, looking North.

deep and beautiful glen leading to the village of La Forest, which is sweetly situated. From hence we pursued the coast road leading to the church of Tortival [*sic*]over an elevated but level and richly cultivated part of the island, yielding luxuriant crops. We obtained frequent glympses [*sic*] of the sea line and French coast. The village of Torteval is small and straggling, but it has a handsome new church just completed, with an elegant light tower and spire. After making a sketch of it, we entered a deep road overhung by trees on either side, which conducted us to the shore of Roquaine [*sic*] bay, remarkable for its castle. It was lowwater, and the rocks with which this part of the coast is girted, presented a most wild and grotesque appearance. The Hanois or Hanway rocks stretched out several miles from Plymont point, very dangerous to navigation. Here the Boreas frigate Capt. Scott was lost in a calm in the year [...] she missed stays and the current set her on; most of the crew perished, and only one officer survived. Amongst the recesses of these formidable rocks, many small vessels find secure anchorage. The coast here like all the rest we had passed, presented a most animated scene from the numerous persons engaged in cutting down and collecting the seaweed which is used both for fuel and manure. Two seasons of

8.   View at St. Martins Point with General Doyle's column, with Sark and the French coast in distance.

the year, Midsummer and Michaelmas are appointed for gathering this useful article, during which time the villages adjoining the coast are for a time deserted. Roquaine castle is built on a massive rock, projecting some distance into the bay. It has nine guns mounted on it, and it is furnished with a martello tower within. The approach is by a ladder. The approach is rocky but the rest of the bay is low and shingley interspersed with rocks. It is defended by batteries and breastworks for musketry connect the whole line. We still continued our track along the beach avoiding the main road that we might have a perfect view of the coast scenery and the walk became more tedious owing to the quantity of weed with which the whole shore at high water mark was covered. It is laid out for the purpose of curing to fit it for fuel, and we were not permitted to walk over it. Le Rhee Barracks, Fort Saumares and Lihou island,[1] which is connected with the main at low water forms the most projecting point on this side of the island. Here we quitted the coast and pursued the military road, cut by General Doyle, leading to St. Pierreport.

About 2 miles from Le Rhee barracks, and near Perelle bay, is a house called the Royal George kept by Monsr. Dumaresqe which offers comfortable accomodation to dining parties. Here we determined to remain for the night if a bed could be procured, which we did not expect from the information received at St. Pierre, we were however provided with one, and a good dinner, which was more immediately necessary. We found the Royal George to be a place of great resort as a dining station for the inhabitants of Peter Port, from which it is distant only five miles. After partaking of a very comfortable meal, which we must particularise, we strolled down to the right battery of the three on Vason [*sic*] bay, and after visiting Richmond barracks on le Crocq point we returned to the inn at 9 o'clock and immediately prepared to take possession of our new apartment, which tho very small delighted us with the prospect of the useful and ornamental.

Wednesday 18th. A serene and sunny morning we rose at 6 o'clock and retraced our steps to the bay of Roquaine in order to complete our sketches on this side (of) the island which the lateness of the hour on the preceeding day would not allow of. We returned to breakfast at 9 o'clock and found a well furnished table, the curds and cream were most excellent and in profusion, and the moderate charge that was made in our bill, for the good fare and great civility we experienced, is worth noticing. The dinner was as follows: A shoulder of lamb, an excellent Jupiter ham, peas, potatoes, and cabbage, pancakes and a large currant dumpling, lots of cream, Orgeat, a large bowl of curds, superlative bread, one bottle of London porter, four glasses cherry bounce, one bottle of old Ruby port, two glasses of brandy, bed, breakfast with a column of Guernsey muffins, curds and nutmeg etc. with deep thirlemeres – damage 9/10. We took leave of our good host and his daughters, with something like regret, and promised him another visit. We continued to trace the coast which is lower on this side of the island than it is on the south but presents the same rocky and formidable appearance. The bays are seen at low water beset with the most terrific masses. Saumarez Fort stands on Le Rhee point, it has a martello tower for great guns, with an outwork. Close to this on the south side of Perelle bay is to be seen a cromlech situated on rising ground close to the waters edge; it is called the Druids' altar: compared with many others, and particularly the one in the Marquis of Anglesea's grounds at Plasnewyd it sinks into insignificance. On the north side of Perelle bay is situated Richmond barracks, capable of containing 500 men. Le Crocq point is the southern boundary of a deep and shallow bay, called Vasson bay, on the north side is another work called [...] commanded by a martello tower in its centre. At a little distance above it are Hommet barracks, capable of containing 200 men. Under Hommet barracks, is a small bay named

9. Torteval Church, S. side Is. Guernsey.

Havre Vasse, and close to it the deep bay of Cobo, which affords two small places of security for boats, amongst it numerous rocks, under the names of Saline bay and Long port, above it towers the signal station called Rock de Guet situated on the crest of a bluff and bold rock commanding all the signal stations of the island. It was at work communicating signals with Vale castle as we passed under it. To the north of this is Grand Rocque, a rugged mass of rocks, projecting into the sea: a work is formed on the most projecting point. The land here is low but varied by large masses of rock, which extend some distance inland and from the appearance of the country the sea must have receded from it. Amongst the masses of rock we observed one of very peculiar appearance, which we named the Guernsey Sphynx. We bent our steps towards it, it forms a singular profile viewing it from the south side. Next come Grand Rocque barracks, with Portinfer and Pulias bays in which we observed some boats amongst the rocks. We now ascended some steep ground leading up to an old Signal Station which commanded a view of the Vale scenery, and the distant islands of Herm and Jethou, the channel however that separated them from us was not visible. Whilst we were admiring the prospect, we observed a large vessel in full sail cutting through the landscape and separating them from us, the light fell strongly upon her sails and formed a curious contrast with the blue aerial tint in the distance. From this point the land falls rapidly towards Grand Havre, a bay which forms a deep indent and runs up close to Le Vale church, it formerly overflowed the whole of the low land of Le Vale, to St. Sampson's harbour, but amongst the many improvements which this island has undergone, whilst under the command of General Doyle, the reclaiming this land and forming a good road over it has been a very prominent one. It is now under good cultivation. We directed our steps towards Le Vale church which is very ancient and still exhibits one window on its east face which though small may be admired for its elegant tracery. In the church yard opposite the west entrance we observed a pile of rocks, which bore the appearance of a cromlech, and which on examination we supposed to have been a Druids altar. It seems to be unnoticed, one end of the covering stone rests on a large pebble placed upon a block of granite. Near to this

10. Peter Port & the Saints Bay with Genl. Doyle's Column and Sark island in distance. South side of island.

-posit, they are brought from the French coast. In this harbour is laid up, the Priva-teer Cutter, belonging to M.r Hallier of Port S.t Peter, which during the war, realised a very large fortune for that gentleman.

We followed the coast road which is strongly defended by lines & Martello towers, the whole way to S.t Peter, a distance of 2½ miles, & arri-ved at Rings British hotel at ½ after 5 o'clock not a little fatigued with our days excursion. we dined, & were glad to retire early to our beds.

Thursday 16.th This day was brought on, not in clouds & storms, tho. it was, great & important; the bells commenced a peal at an early hour, & an infinite number of wreaths & crowns, for-med of flowers, were fixed over the doors, & sus-pended across the streets; it was a day of jubilee & cajolery, & not a more serene or lovely one ever dawned, to grace the pageant at-

11. Pleinmont point, Rocquaine Bay & Castle part of the Hannoy Rocks.

church are a few good houses and a considerable quantity of wood adorns the road side to St. Sampson's harbour. This is a dry harbour, but the most secure place in the island; its entrance is from the east, it has lately been much improved by the States and they are now erecting a pier and sea wall to render it more secure for the oyster fishery which has lately been established here. We saw the beds prepared for their deposit. They are brought from the French coast. In this harbour is laid up the privateer cutter belonging to a Mr. Hallier of Port St. Peter which during the war realised a very large fortune for that gentleman.

We followed the coast road which is strongly defended by lines and Martello towers, the whole way to St. Peter, a distance of 2½ miles and arrived at Kings British hotel at ½ after 5 o'clock not a little fatigued with our days excursion. We dined and were glad to retire early to our beds.

Thursday 19th. This day was brought on, not in clouds and storms, tho, it was great and important. The bells commenced a peal at an early hour, and an infinite number of wreaths and crowns, formed of flowers, were fixed over the doors, and suspended across the streets; it was a day of jubilee and cajolery, and tendant on the coronation of a King.

A public déjeunée in the open air was given
to the Officers of the 12th & all the troops in the
island, consisting of the 12th of the line, and the
different militias, were paraded on a spacious
promenade, called the New ground, & after marching in review, were drawn up on the beach,
& pier of the harbour, ready to fire a feu de joye
at 12 oclock. We thought this a favorable opportunity for seeing the beauty of the place
& we sallied out to enjoy the scene. Every street
was crowded with well dressed persons, & the
effect when we arrived on the new ground, was
very striking. We found it a Vauxhall in miniature: a spacious green, surrounded with
fine grown elm trees, was covered with the
troops & spectators; spacious gravel walks, wide
enough for two carriages to pass each other,
conducted us amongst the trees, & here the

not a more serene or lovely one ever dawned to grace the pageant attendant on the coronation of a King.

A public dejeunee in the open air was given to the Officers of the 12th and all the troops in the island consisting of the 12th of the line, and the different militias, were paraded on a spacious promenade called the New ground, and after marching in review, were drawn up on the beach and pier of the harbour, ready to fire a feu de joye at 12 o'clock. We thought this a favorable opportunity for seeing the beauty of the place and we sallied out to enjoy the scene. Every street was crowded with well dressed persons, and the effect when we arrived on the new ground was very striking. We found it a Vauxhall in miniature a spacious green surrounded with fine grown elm trees was covered with the troops and spectators; spacious gravel walks wide enough for two carriages to pass each other, conducted us amongst the trees, and here the groupes [*sic*] of young people that met the eye in every direction, led us to imagine the whole population of the island assembled on this occasion. Where any opening presented itself among the branches, the distant sea of the clearest azure with the picturesque rocks of Sark, Herme, and Jettou, delighted the eye.

Whilst we were enjoying this charming scene and the pure air of this delightful spot, we were occasionally engaged with scrutinising eye in taking a fair average of the beauty about us, it was of tolerable quality but we thought it would have appeared more captivating had it been disencumbered of some of the finery which bedecked it in profusion. Whilst thus engaged we stumbled upon an old acquaintance Captn. Fisher, who recognised us immediately tho. it was 12 or 14 years since two of the party met before. He is a native of the place and we were obliged to him for his offer of becoming our Ciceroni. After viewing all the sights we accompanied him to his house, and were introduced to Mrs. F. whom one of us had slightly known during her stay in Wigan in 1814. She is a Yorkshire lady and was married at that period; she made many enquiries after her friends and particularly the Leeches. At ½ after 11 o'clock we took our leave of Mrs. F. and accompanied Capt. F. to see the exhibition in the town and harbour.

It was commenced at 12 o'clock by three rounds fired from the different batteries on the right and left of the town, between them the feu de joye of the troops, had a pretty effect, being flanked by six field pieces, which distinguished and divided the musketry. At 1 o'clock his Majesty's frigate Tyne and Mr. Pelham's brig yacht Falcon, fired a salute; they had arrived the day before, and were gaily decked out with colours. Afterwards Capt. F. took us into the country to show us the villas of different gentlemen, and we dined at a place called the King's Mills, it was a feast of the eye only, for our fare was very humble, bacon and eggs was all we could procure, which we washed down with good raspberry brandy.

the groupes of young people that met the eye
in every direction, led us to imagine the whole
population of the island assembled on this occa
-sion. Where any opening presented itself a
-mong the branches, the distant sea of the clea
-rest azure, with the picturesque rocks of Sark
Herme, & Jettou, delighted the eye.
Whilst we were enjoying this charming scene
& the pure air of this delightful spot, we were
occasionally engaged with scrutinising eye in
taking a fair average of the beauty about us:
it was of tolerable quality, but we thought
it would have appeared more captivating,
had it been disencumbered of some of the finery
which bedecked it in profusion. Whilst they
engaged we stumbled upon an old acquain-
-tance Capt.n Fisher, who recognised us imme-
-diately th.o it was 12 or 14 years since two of
the party met before. He is a native of the

12. Signal Station on the Rock de Guet, West Coast of Guernsey.

We pursued a different route home thro the fields, and presently entered a thickly wooded valley called the Grouanier. In this shady retired spot and near the centre of it, we found the residence of Major Laine, formerly of the 44th Regt. He has lately purchased this property for which he paid £2,000. Here we might have supposed ourselves one thousand miles from the sea, had we not here and there discovered it thro the dark rich foliage which surrounded us. The pleasure grounds are beautiful, roses, cammellias, hydrangiums, and rhododendrons were found in every part, growing freely and attaining a large size, and were so beautifully arranged and managed, that we might have supposed them flourishing in their natural climate. Capt. F. being known to the owner of this delightful place sent word that we were rambling through his grounds, when he immediately came out to meet us, and conducted us to the house, where we joined the family in a most sociable cup of tea.

The evening was now far advanced and we took our leave of the ladies, the Major however, gave us the pleasure of his company part of the way to town. He is a most agreeable little man about 40, an Irishman by birth, and married to a daughter of Mr. Mesurier Governor of Sark, by whom he has a family of 3 or 4 children. The town of St. Peter Port presented a most splendid appearance on

ed the day before, & were gaily decked out
with colours. Afterwards Capt.ⁿ F took us into
the country, to shew us the villas of different
gentlemen, & we dined at a place called the
Kings Mills; it was a feast of the eye only
for our fare was very humble, bacon & eggs
was all we could procure, which we washed
down with good raspberry brandy.—
We pursued a different route home thr.º the
fields, & presently entered a thickly wooded
valley called the Grouanier. In this shady
retired spot, & near the centre of it, we found
the residence of Major Laine, formerly of the
44.ᵗʰ Reg.ᵗ he has lately purchased this proper-
-ty for which he paid £2000. Here we might
have supposed ourselves one thousand miles
from the sea, had we not here & there disco-
-vered it thr.º the dark rich foliage which sur-
-rounded us. The pleasure grounds are beautiful

our approach, being completely illuminated and from the circumstances of every house having so many windows filled with the best glass, it had a most brilliant effect. Fireworks were displayed from the many different eminences and we observed them rising as tho out of the sea from on board the Tyne frigate and Mr. Pelhams yacht. The streets were almost impassable from the crowd of well dressed people and we observed many individuals of the Militia Regmt. returning homewards in different directions exhibiting convincing proof of their loyalty and attachment to the good old cause. Here indeed unanimity has hitherto prevailed and the detested breath of radicalism had not yet polluted this happy soil.

We retired to rest at an early hour leaving the enjoyment of this gay scene to the young and less experienced.

Friday 20th. We passed in visiting the coast scenery and the adjacent parishes of St. Martin's la Forest, St. André & St. Saviour; we dined at our old quarters Dumaresque's Hotel, the shortest distance from hence to the town is only five miles over an excellent road commanding views of the N.W. coast and many gentlemen's seats. It is a favorite drive to the Royal George which is much

13. Inn kept by Monsr. Dumaresque called Royal George.

frequented during the summer months by parties, who by giving a day's notice can have a comfortable dinner provided for them. This house and another kept by Alexandre are the only two where accomodation can be met with. We returned to the capital at 8 o'clock and enjoyed a bottle of perry and some of the liqueur for which this place is faimed.

Saturday 21st. This is the market day of Port St. Peter, and we passed an hour in looking over the supplies.[2] The fish market was abundantly supplied with shell fish and we noticed particularly the spider crab, so called from its resemblance to that insect, it was here of considerable size and in abundance. This and the common crab exceed in size the largest we had ever seen in the London market, and sold at 10p. each. Crawfish & lobsters were plentiful and large. Bream and Bass with a variety of other fish were sold equally cheap, but Soles and Plaice maintain the prices of England. At 10 o'clock we set out to visit that part of the island we had not yet seen and passing by Vale church which we had visited before, directed our steps towards Lancress bay on the north coast, and looked over the different works erected for its defence. Here within the compass perhaps of two miles we gained a view of six Martello towers of the fifteen which are erected on the shores and bays of this island. The coast in this part does not present anything different to what we had already seen. From Doyles battery which stands on the most northern point of the island, we obtained a good view of the entrance into the Little Russel, and the opposite point of Herm island which is low and sandy compassed with many rocks. We pursued the coast passing the island of Homette bennêst. The land to the south of it is lower than any of the rest, but of the same character rocky and dangerous. Havre de Bourdeaux lies under Vale Castle on the north side, and affords shelter to many small fishing boats; it is dry at low water. We returned to town at 3 o'clock by Sampson's harbour being engaged to dine with Capt. Fisher; we met at table Major Laing and another gentleman and passed an extremely pleasant evening; we had a variety of wines and returned to our quarters a little before 12 o'clock, merry and wise.

Sunday 22nd. This morning we indulged a little longer in bed than usual and after breakfast attended Divine Service. A sermon in French and English was read by the Revd. Monsr. Navet. It was a short eulogium on St. Mary Magdalene. There is only one small chapel on the island and it is situated in an obscure part of the town called Rosemary Lane. Service is performed twice on Sundays by the same gentleman at the hours of 10 and 12 o'clock. The established religion is protestant but the Methodists and other sects appear to be increasing rapidly in number. We were informed that there is not a resident Catholic family in the island. Capt. Fisher called upon us at 12 o'clock in order to introduce us to his brother in law, Mr. McCulloch who has a good collection of shells peculiar to the shores of these islands of which he informed us there were 133 different

14.   Vale Castle with Port St. Peter and Fort George in distance.

sorts. He has also a few good paintings and drawings, two or three executed by Mr. Young the artist, spoken of before as a passenger with us in the packet. Capt. Fisher afterwards conducted us thro. the Hospital or poor house which is a most complete establishment, having many conveniences within itself, such as a bakery, brewhouse, school etc. A partition wall devides the building into two parts, one half is destined for the education of orphan girls, until they attain an age that will enable them to go out to service. There were between 40 & 50 of them in number. The whole establishment is remarkable for its cleanliness.

We visited two cells that were occupied by two deranged females; one was old and extremely noisy, we found her seated in bed. The other was young not being more than 24. She was pacing her cell with her arms folded and her hair dishevelled. She looked extremely pale and interesting, her features indeed were lovely and we were informed that she had been considered the prettiest girl in the town; we did not learn the cause of her unfortunate situation. Quitting this sorrowful scene, we visited the garden of Mr. Lucas situated in the higher part of the town. He has a good sized green-house and we observed the vines, well loaded with fruit, which is here obtained without much cost of fire, a little only being used when the vines first begin to push, in order to forward them at that season; the natural heat is afterwards quite sufficient to bring the fruit to maturity. Mr. Lucas had a barrel of Brazil earth, left in his possession by Bonpland one of the superintendants of the Jardin des Plantes at Paris, who touched here on his return to France. It was a little damaged by salt water and was not thought worth the carriage home. Mr. L. had put the earth into pots and boxes and many young plants had sprung up from the seed contained in the soil. We understand that earth is frequently brought over for this purpose and that valuable and strong plants are thus sometimes procured. We observed amongst them a fine Palma Christi and two of the Mimosa tribe. Mr. Lucas politely offered to accompany us to see the house and garden of Mr. Pierse formerly a linen draper in London, who retired to this island and built himself a complete box au citoyen, finished at a great expense and with some taste. The greenhouse contains the finest Camellias in the island; we observed here as well as many other places, the green and variegated aloes, one had taken root in an old wall, affording a convincing proof of the mildness of the winters in these islands.

15.   Cornet Castle with Isles Herm & Jethou taken under the Works of Fort George.

We passed many very excellent houses in the higher part of the town charmingly situated, most of which command extensive sea views and are sheltered from the prevailing winds with flourishing plantations and adorned with many varieties of fine evergreens which here thrive exceedingly. We returned to dinner at 4 o'clock a meal which we generally took at Marshal's hotel where the Sarnian Club have two reading rooms to which we had access thro the kindness of our friend Captn. Fisher.

We passed the evening in his company, he took us to a farm house in the neighbourhood, where he pointed out a stone fixed over the door bearing on a brass plate some heraldic quarterings. We observed two Griffins, and the date 1213 underneath, the farmer whose name was Du Frize informed us that his family had come over to England with William the Conqueror and had afterwards returned to this island, which may not be impossible, nor perhaps improbable as the farms here are tenanted by the real proprietors, and descend in a continued succession from father to son, a custom which prevails generally throughout the island. We retired to bed at 10 o'clock when according to an old saying 'we slept without rocking'.

Monday 23rd. We visited the environs of the town which has much picturesque scenery to admire; and afterwards went thru the parishes of St. Martin's La Forest, St. Peters, St. Saviour and St. Andre, and dined again at Dumaresque's. The island is sufficiently diversified without being hilly, and is in the highest state of cultivation, it abounds with numerous and extensive orchards, we observed that almost every farm house has a fig tree, some of these were extremely large. They are trained low and spreading and are supported by props, in common seasons they yield abundantly. One near the church of St. Andre overhangs the road and was loaded with fruit. A low stone wall forms the common fence of the country where wood does not abound, on the top of which is laid three coverings of sods and a little soil; gorse seed is then sown which in the course of two or three years, grows up into an impervious fence. It is a most valuable article of fuel, and is one of the sources of profit to the farmer. Cattle during the summer months are pastured on the richest crops of clover. They are fastened by head ropes until they have consumed what is within their reach, and in this manner the whole field is regularly cropped without any waste.[3] The milk and butter is proverbially rich and good. We returned to our quarters about 9 o'clock and after a dose of creme de Framboise as a nightcap, we marched up into the attics and passed the countersign bon soir.

Tuesday 24th. We rambled out after breakfast to the heights of St. George and visited Clarence battery on the lowermost projecting point, we also looked through the stores where the gun carriages, Levers, Rammers, Sponges and a Harness for ye horse Artillery etc. is kept in the most complete and admirable

16. St. Sampsons Church & Harbour, Martello tower on Mt. Crevet & Sark in the distance.

order. We passed by the Artillery barracks which are situated on the edge of the cliff shut out by the heights and fortifications except to the Eastward, in which direction they have a commanding view of the island of Jersey, Great & Little Sark etc. with the French coast. Under St. Martin's point is the small but deep sandy bay of Fermain, commanded by batteries from different heights; these are connected by breastworks for musketry. In the ravine on Fermain bay stands No.15 Martello tower.

It had kept very fine all the morning, but the wind blew hard from the W.S.W. at 12 o'clock the clouds began to lower and obscured the sea from our view, we thought this a sufficient warning to retrace our steps homewards, but we were overtaken by the storm which came on with sharp squalls of wind and rain which continued without intermission till 8 o'clock. We devoted the rest of the day to our journals and passed the evening at the reading room. Whilst at dinner we observed two or three vessels come to anchor in the roads and the sea foaming on the rocks under our window, presented a different scene to what we had been accustomed to behold. This was the first day since our departure from Liverpool that we had experienced any inconvenience or detention from the weather. The streets of Port St. Pierre are very steep having only one channel formed in the centre of each; the torrent of water in heavy rains becomes very great particularly near the foot of High St. where the waters from the different streets unite, and fall into the harbour carrying away in their rapid course whatever filth they meet with. This was another market day. There was an excellent supply of various sorts of fish and mackerels were selling, quite fresh caught, at 8 for 1/-. We broached another bottle of Madame Chassevent A.C. Premiere qualite, to counteract the affects of the damp atmospheres and we resolved on carrying off with us two of her ladyship's eleves, for the judgement of our friends at Liverpool; they are very agreeable and enlivening companions. We took leave of bon Madame at 10 o'clock and swivelled into our couches.

Wednesday 25th. We amused ourselves during the morning in rambling about and furnishing our sketch books; it continued to blow very hard at S. West. The anchorage of Port St. Pierre was quiet but the passage of the Little Russel thro which the tide sets strong, was much ruffled.

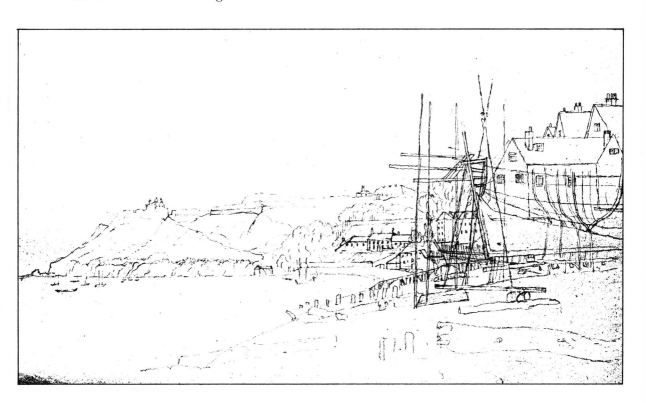

17. St. George's Works & part of Bay St. Peter Port Guernsey, showing Building Yard there.

In the course of the day we visited the Courthouse, a good building and conveniently fitted up; in the court room there is a whole length portrait of the late Governor General Doyle in his full uniform, a fine painting. The Greffier then conducted us to a room where the records are preserved. Here we were shown a Papal Bull, dated Aug.1486 it declares excommunication against all those who shall ill treat the inhabitants of these islands; another order from King Charles of France, for all the Bulls to be publicly read in all the islands, several Charters; one of Richard the 2nd dated 28th July 1395 signed Hereil Pole, others of Elizabeth, James and Charles, the former one was finely emblazoned and was in very great preservation. A letter from the Bishop of Coutances addressed to the clergy of these islands, and dated 12th July 1565 signed D. Cosse de Coutances. We then visited the gaol where, to the honor of the island, we only found one prisoner, who had been committed for stabbing a soldier. He was undergoing his sentence which was only three months imprisonment. Afterwards, accompanied by our friend Capt. Fisher, we visited the gardens of Monsr. Le Serre and Mr. Mourant where we saw some good glass. We observed that the hothouses here have only one flue running through the centre of the house. Geraniums are a favorite flower with the Gentry, and many new varieties are annually raised. Mr. Mourant had presented the horticultural Society of London with a fine new specimen last year.

In this garden we observed a very large plant of the variegated aloe growing out of the wall; it was supported underneath by a small stone wall. Two very large orange trees were also trained against the wall 15 feet in height; one of them bore a very fine crop of fruit, some nearly ready to gather, and of a large size. They are slightly protected during the winter months. The Gladiolus, Verbena, Camellia and Budlia globora are common in most gardens; the Verbena has been known to attain the height of 20 feet and upwards, spreading in a circle of a diameter equal to its height, and its long branches reaching down to the ground on all sides. A few other plants of tender constitution in England may be enumerated which appear equally hardy in this more uniform climate, such as the Celtis micrantha, Camellia japonnica, some species of the Olea and Proteas, with many species of the genus Cistus; the Yucca aloifolia, Dracocephalum Canariense, Jasminum Azoricum Nerium cleander, Clethra arborea, Daphne odorata, Mimulus glutinosus, Correa alba, Malaleuca Hypericifiolia Gorteria regens, and several others. We finished our excursion by seeing Mr. Dobrees' House and gardens. This gentleman is uncle to Captn. Fisher The house has one of the best situations for command of prospect and richness of soil. On our return to our lodgings, Mr. Brock the Bailiff and chief magistrate called upon us and invited us to breakfast the next morning at his country house. At ½ after 4 o'clock we dined again with our friend Captn. Fisher and passed a very pleasant evening. A Mr. Ambrose joined us at tea: We returned home at 11 o'clock without any assistance, tho we had plied the port and cherry brandy with unsparing hand.

Thursday 26th. Our friend Capt. F. waited on us this morning at ½ after 7 o'clock and we walked out to breakfast with Mr. Brock; he is brother to the late Major General Brock who was killed at Canada and he had another brother who fell at [...] After the breakfast things were removed there was abundance of fruit and the richest of cream placed on the table; the grounds command the finest views of the bay and islands. At 12 o'clock Mr. B. returned with us to town. He is said to be a shrewd and clever man. He was formerly in business in this place but sustained heavy losses. His greatest however was said to arise from an imprudent marriage with a woman in a very inferior situation by whom he has a family of eight children. She never appears at table when strangers are present. We called on the captain of the Prince Bouillon, Jersey packet, and he informed us he was sailing at ½ after six o'clock the following morning for Jersey. We therefore arranged everything to go with him. Capt. Fischer [*sic*] determined to accompany us and pass a week with us in the island. We called to take leave of Mrs. F. from whom we had received much civility and who pressed us to remain that we might have an opportunity of judging of the beauty of Guernsey at an assembly which was to take place the following evening. We returned to town to dinner. The island of Guernsey is small being only [...] miles in length and averaging about 6 in breadth. Its population by a census taken whilst we were there, amounts to 21,000 including the Isles of Sark etc. The town and parish of Port St. Peter alone comprises 11,000. The neighbouring island of Sark contains 488, Herm 28 and Jethou 8.[4] On the shore of this island we found growing abundantly, the Sea holly, Yellow horned poppy, Convolvulus, yellow wallflower, purple and scarlet stock, Cammomile and fennel, and in some places particularly the deep glen leading from Petit Bo bay to La Forçet we observed the wild peppermint. This island came into possession of the English with William the conqueror, and is supposed to have been first occupied by French fishermen who came to cure the fish caught on its shores. A fort called Sellerie [*sic*], or salting place on the north side of the town is supposed to have been one of the stations, and St Sampson's harbour another. It is said to have been once entirely covered with wood. The Guernsey Elm is the common tree of the island. There are also the English varieties, and the Canada elm, which is of very quick growth. The oak and sycamore also flourish. Innumerable evergreens ornament every rustic cottage and attain to a very large size. The rock on the shores is of the purest granite and it is found in many places of the interior, forming a most desirable building material. Labour is moderately low, the wages of workmen being about 2/4 p diem.

Guernsey commands an extensive trade and has nearly 70 vessels belonging to its port, trading to Holland, South America, British America and the Baltic. Three arrivals from Buenos Ayres occurred whilst we were here, the Dutch and French take a great part of their imports and in return supply them with wine and corn.

18. St. Sampson's Harbour, Mt. Crevet and part of Sark I. in the distance.

Five large vessels were on the stocks, one coppered & ready to launch in a few days. Some of these are built on stages elevated five feet or more from the ground, and extending probably 50 feet on to the shores of the bay. Others are launched across the streets which run so near the shore at a place called Glatney, as to be sometimes washed by the sea. There are public warm and cold baths at Port St. Peter, two or three news rooms and reading rooms and tho no great show is made by the inhabitants in the way of splendid equipages or establishments we were assured that they possess in the English Funds a sum exceeding £2,000,000, besides other investments in the French funds. The land is extremely well cultivated chiefly under wheat, and we observed many fields of parsnips, clover and beet. The potatoe is also much grown always intermixed with patches of beans and cabbages. The island however does not produce corn for more than four months consumption. There are several Druidical remains on the coast, all of which are of small dimensions compared with many others. We noticed one in the church yard of Le Vale church immediately opposite the door of the west entrance; they are all close to the shores.

The island of Sark which is only three miles distant from Port St. Peter is worth a visit and parties frequently make excursions to it, the cliffs are stupendously high affording more romantic scenery than Guernsey, many shells are found on its shores. Herme is the property of Col. Lindsay, brother to the Earl of Balcarras; he purchased it from Government for the sum of £6000 and at present resides on it. There are several signal stations on the island of Guernsey, which have all a communication from one to the other, and no vessel can approach the coast without being discovered and her description known immediately at Port St. Peter. The telegraph is a pole with a yard rigged across to which is seized several small blocks and between the blocks ropes lead down to the ground and are secured there. Bags stuffed with straw or any other material are hoisted by means of the blocks, and traverse on the ropes by which they are kept steady; these denote the number of vessels in sight, for the follwing explanation we are indebted to our friend Captn. Fisher.

This signal denotes two cutters making for the island from the Southward. The number of balls on the higher yard denotes the number of vessels. A pendant above that, the vessel is a cutter, or any fore and aft rigged vessel, A Budgie is hoisted for a square rigged vessel & square red flag for men of war. The lower yard serves to denote the point of the compass the vessel comes from.

1 South - 2 East - 3 West - 4 North, which last mark always remains fixed.

When a vessel is passing by one ball only is hoisted on the lower bar and 2 if making for the island. Should a fleet heave in sight, consisting of different rigged vessels, then the classes it consists of are denoted on the flag staff, and every ball on the upper yard expresses 10 vessels, and if there are more brigs than any other description of square rigged vessels in the fleet, the Budgie is hoisted over the other two colours, if cutters, the pendant, and if men of war, the square red flag.

The peasantry of Guernsey are remarkably civil to strangers, and seldom pass by without some mark of respect. They are a hardy industrious people, the language they speak is a gibberish bearing more resemblance certainly to the French than any other and differing from it perhaps more in pronounciation than in the structure. Most of the farmers understand English and a person is seldom at a loss on that account in passing thro the country. The society in Port St. Peter is divided into three classes, composed of the Gentry, Tradesmen and shopkeepers. There is no advancing beyond the circle in which you have been accustomed to move in early life, whatever pretensions, fortune or the advantage of education may have given you The Assemblies held here are of course particularly select, and a stranger can only gain admission to them by being known and introduced by some respectable person. Admission to them is a certain criterion of your frequenting the best society. Some of the richest merchants in the place find themselves excluded. In Port St. Peter there is a free school, founded and endowed by Elizabeth over the entrance door is carved the arms of [...] The funds appear to amount to about £200 per ann; it is under the management of the curate of St. Martin's who employs the curate of St. Andrew's to do the work. Latin is the only dead language taught. There is to be seen in Glatney street on the north side of the town some few remains of the front of an ancient abbey consisting of the gateway and carved work over it, but we could learn no particulars of it.[5]

Friday 27th. We embarked at ½ after 6 o'clock this morning with Captn. Fischer on board the Prince Bouillon packet, Captn. Bichard. She is a small vessel of only 30 tons. The packet from England arrived about 6 o'clock and was lying too in the roads waiting the mail for Jersey. We found about 30 passengers aboard the Prince Bouillon, mostly women. The wind was fair and it had moderated during the night, but there was a heavy swell, which very soon brought on the usual incontestible proofs of indisposition amongst the passengers. It was a busy time for the steward who had two mops in commission. The distance from land to land between the islands is 21 miles and about 30 from the pierheads. The islands of the two Sarks, Herme and Jethou and Le Marchand and appear on the left hand and the French coast on the right. When the rock Le Tocq, which lies off Sark, is shut in with that island, the passage is considered half accomplished.

By 10 o'clock we were abreast of the rock named La Corbiere, the southernmost point of the island and coasted close along the shore for about 6 miles untill the deep and magnificent bay of St. Aubin opened to our view with its picturesque and lovely banks. On the northeast side of this bay is placed the town of St. Helier and opposite to it in the other recess of the bay that of St. Aubin. The shores appear a white firm sand.

We quickly approached Elizabeth castle, opposite the entrance of the harbour. It is built on rocks which stretch out some distance into ye bay and it can be approached at half ebb or earlier by a good road formed of shingle. This castle commands the whole of the bay. At 12 o'clock we came to anchor under its walls, as it was low water, and landed in the boat. We were conducted in a similar manner as when we landed at Port St. Peter, to Deals Hotel, where we breakfasted & immediately after set out in search of lodgings, determined to make arrangements for taking all our meals there instead of going to the Inn for them. In this we found some difficulty as we were three in number to provide for. We at last succeeded at Mrs. Viel's in Charing Cross. We visited the heights and works over the town and dining at 6 o'clock we retired early to rest.

19. Bay of St. Aubins with Elizabeth Castle and Hermitage Rock.

Saturday 28th. This proved a determined wet day & unfortunately it was market day, we were supplied however with an umbrella by Miss Viel and set out to view the display made for the Jersias. At the market place we found ourselves sheltered from the weather; the stalls and flagged walks for passengers are roofed over but there are also spacious gravel walks between ye stalls so that you may have the advantage of either sun or shade. The building forms three sides of an oblong square, in the area are four other rows of buildings divided from each other by broad gravel walks, wide enough to allow two carts to pass each other. One wing of this building is appropriated to the butter market, the corresponding one for fish and the buildings in the area for meat shambles, the centre is used for fruit vegetables etc. It was tolerably well supplied but fish was scarce and dearer much, than in Guernsey. Butter and meat were rather lower, the former sold at 10d and the latter, which made a beautiful and tempting display at 7d. We made our purchases for the supply of our table consisting of a fine pair of soles, wg. perhaps 4lbs for which we paid 2/- and a part of a sirloin of beef wg. 7 lbs. @ 7d. We were directed to a confectioner by the name of Bolton in the square for a variety of wines, which might be purchased in any quantity even a bottle Claret as low as 7/6 per doz. and port wine @22/6. We ordered some port and Lisbon wine, and a substantial fruit pie to be sent to our lodgings.

The Court was sitting this day to decide on the validity of a late election of a chief magistrate; we walked in; the bench of magistrates were clothed in their robes of scarlet faced with black velvet. The pleadings were carried forward in French which we could not understand, being prevented by the crowd of persons from approaching near enough. At 3 o'clock it cleared up and we walked thro the town which is well built and the streets are capacious and well paved. It is situated on level ground and makes no appearance from the bay as you approach it, being shut out by the fortified heights above it. In the square is a statue of Charles the second in bronze raised on a pedestal of granite about 10 or 12 feet in height. This is a spacious airy part of the town and being well flagged forms a principal promenade. It was in the square that the French formed their troops after having effected their landing during the night near St. Clements point, in Jany 1781. Major Pearson who commanded, fell in the moment of victory and flower of his youth, being only 24 years of age, he was buried in the church close to scene of action a handsome monument is erected to his memory having the following inscription

In memory of Major Robert Pearson
who
when the island was invaded by ye French
Fell bravely fighting
At the head of the British and Island troops
He died in the flower of youth
And in the moment of Victory
On the 6th day of Jany
1781 aged 24
The States of the Island
In grateful testimony of their deliverance
Caused this monument to be erected
at the public expence

Baron Rulecourt who commanded the French forces on this occasion was also mortally wounded and died. Our friend Mr. Leigh has a good print of the attack and death of Major Pearson in which the statue of Charles and the town Hall are shown; two houses in the square still bear numerous marks of the grape shot received on that occasion.[6]

We dined at 5 o'clock. and as the evening was fine we strolled into the country towards the church of St. Saviour. We found the old roads very narrow and deep, and so filled with trees that it is difficult to get a sight of the sky. The new roads are much more commodious and open and are kept in very good repair. The church of St. Saviour is large and has a good square tower. It is situated at the head of a pretty vale and commands fine prospects of the sea and the town and works above it. We returned home passing by the house of Col. Touzell who

20. The town of St. Helier with the fortified height of Mont de la Ville and the newly constructed Regent's Fort.

is now inspector of Militias, and Military Secretary. This gentleman was formerly quartered in Wigan, where thro. the interest of Lord Balcarras, he was appointed Adjutant and trained the Militia there. He married a sister of Mr. Moulson of that town. We returned home before 9 o'clock and attended in the square to hear the Bugles of the 12th Regt. quartered here; they play extremely well and attract a numerous company every evening.

Sunday 29th. After breakfast we attended chapel at 10 o'clock. There are two services performed here, the first at 8 o'clock. Messrs. [...] do the duty, There is only one chapel on ye island, but the number of Catholics exceed those of Guernsey, but they are all strangers French and a few Irish; we observed 53 rank and file of the 12th Regt. amongst the number. We dined at 4 o'clock on an excellent sirloin of beef and after a glass of wine a bon marche. We walked into the country through cross roads, which the sun never visits from the height of the trees and hedges. We returned home thru the beautiful wooded valley of Le Veaux which is seen in its original simplicity. This valley which joins up to the main road about one mile from St. Helier commands from the higher part, picturesque views of the town, the fortified heights and the sea. We arrived in time to hear the bugles of the 12th Infantry play the tattoo and after a glass of Cinq fruits, we sunk on our pillows to sleep.

Monday July 30th. We had intended this day to commence our coast tour of the island, but unfortunately the morning set in with a lowering sky which soon turned to rain, our time was therefore devoted partly to our friends in England and to noting down in our journal the different occurences that had transpired. A temporary gleam of sun enduced us to take a walk to the pier and round the precincts of the town and we left our cards with Brigade Major Treeves, for the acting Governor Col. Touzell. General Gordon had just resigned his command on promotion. He embarked this morning at Orgueil Castle for England, on his leaving St. Helier at an early hour. We heard the guns of Elizabeth Castle salute him. We dined at 4 o'clock and filled up the remainder of the evening in reading the history of Jersey which we obtained a sight of thru the interest of our friend Captn. Fisher. Of the three publications, which we had before us, we considered the one by J. Stead entitled Cabarea [*sic*], to give the best insight into the localities of the island. It is printed in four parts. After a day passed most agreeably we retired to gain fresh vigour for the fatigues of the next.

Tuesday July 31st This morning at 8 o'clock we at length set out on our threatened tour along the shores of the island. We passed by the barracks of the Engineers, and taking the coast road leading along the deep sandy bay of Havre de Pas, beset with innumerable rocks stretching a great distance into the sea, by which the bay is rendered quite inaccessible, it is bounded on the East by the bold rocks of La Motte, seperated at high water from the main. This is a station for many small boats, the shore being bold and shingly. Havre du Hoc and the Greve of St. Clement now opened upon us, defended by its martello towers and works and stretching as far as the point of La Roque, where the rocks again run far into the sea. On the most prominent of these is built a martello tower for artillery called La Croix de feu, or Iron Cross.

It is on this side the French are said to have effected a landing in 1781, but from the most accurate information we could procure from a person residing on the spot at the time, we ascertained that it was on the East side of La Roque where the rocks open a more easy access. Opposite the very spot where the French landed there is a house occupied by Richard Bertram who informed us he was 13 years of age at the time and he pointed out the spot where the boats pulled up. We remarked on the pillars of his gate the date 1781; the house appeared much more ancient. Since that period Seymour tower has been erected as an additional defence. It is placed on a reef of rocks 2 miles from the main. The interior of the country presented a richly wooded appearance interspersed with many beautiful villas and the castle of Orgueil proudly reared its majestic walls over the landscape. Verclut fort was also conspicuous, being situated on very high ground commanding the main road and adjacent country. Here was a signal station which was kept up during the war to communicate with that of Orgeuil castle. The extended bay of Grouville now presented itself with its flat sandy shore nearly free from the rocks so common to the coast of

21. View of St. Clements Bay and point just on the other side of which No. 1 The French landed in 1781.

these islands; we observed many boats employed in dredging for oysters on the banks, situated off this bay. It is defended by six Martello towers and two redoubts. We approached the venerable castle of Mont Orgeuil, built on a towering rock, situated at the North eastern extreme of the bay. It is of very ancient date, and is now partly in ruin. It was the residence of the Prince de Bouillon, whilst he had the command of the squadron stationed off these islands as late as 1801. We ascended its lofty tower and viewed the rooms that Charles the 2nd occupied whilst he was besieged by the Parliamentary forces. These rooms are kept in good repair, and consist of a suite of three apartments, they were used during the late war as barrack rooms for the Officers. The sally port was pointed out to us through which Charles is said to have escaped when he made his way over to France and joined his mother Henrietta. There is at present only a serjeants guard kept up consisting of 7 men and a serjeant of Artillery, and we understood that the board of ordnance do not intend to keep the castle any longer in repair, except the rooms where Charles resided. We observed over the portal leading to the Keep, three escutcheons, the centre bearing the date of 1593, with the motto Gardez la foi. On the summit of the Keep were mounted 5 guns, pointed on the land and harbour side. From this lofty station the very favorable state of the weather enabled us to see the houses and cornfields of the opposite French coast, the cathedral of Coutances was very distinct, the distance over is about 18 miles. A chain of uninhabited rocks lie about a third of the distance between this and the French coast. The small harbour of Goree formed by the rocks of the castle has lately become a station for the oyster fishery which is said to bring in £40,000 annually to this island. The states are at present erecting a very handsome and substantial pier in order to render it more secure. Oyster beds are fitted here for the reception of the fish and not less than 350 sail of boats find employment during the season. The land rises boldly on the north side of the harbour and a convenient road has been formed by shelving down the steep bank which communicates with the pier. The country bordering on the shore is richly wooded and presents many delightful situations for cottages and marine villas. It is much frequented by strangers and several English families have established their quarters in this neighbourhood.

There is nothing known of the foundation of Orgeuil castle except from tradition; it is said to have been built 15 years before our Saviour and occupied the space of 15 years in the building. We returned to St. Helier by the high road leading thru the village of Grouville which has much picturesque scenery and we arrived at our quarters for dinner at ½ after 5 o'clock and were glad to retire early to bed.

Wednesday August 1st. We set out this day at 7 o'clock having ascertained the day before in passing through the village of Grouville that we could be provided with breakfast there. The church of Grouville has a singular spire and the three East windows are large and filled with handsome tracery in which we perceived some stained glass. In the church yard we read the following inscription on a tombstone.

In hopes of a blessed resurrection
near this place are deposited
the remains
of
John Hunter.
William McCulloch
James Reid
Alexr. McKichney
Robert Walker and John Wilson
Grenadiers of the 83rd. Regt. who in a party led on by Lieutenant James Robertson
Against a detachment of the French troops that had invaded this Island gloriously fell
in the midst of their victorious companions at La Roque plate
on the 6th January 1781
To the memory of these brave men
the principal inhabitants of this parish erected this monument

After making a sketch of this church, we pursued a part of the route of yesterday passing by Goree harbour and Orgeuil castle, then along the southern coast which is everywhere bounded by high and rocky land. St. Catherine's bay first presents itself where many small fishing boats are to be seen, a martello tower is erected on a rock projecting into this bay and it is defended by many guns masked on the sides of the surrounding heights. The land here tho hilly is covered with wood amongst which there are many orchards. Verclut is the projecting point on the East, which commands a view of the north side of Orgeuil castle. It has not so imposing an appearance on this flank as when viewed from Grouville. The walk was here intricate and extremely difficult from the coast being so rugged and indented. The small harbour of Fliquet is formed by a conical shaped point of land stretching into the sea to the northward of Verclut; it is rocky and can be approached by yawls only which are drawn up the beach with capstans. On the point of La Coupe are two works, a guard house and watch tower, close to these is the remains of a druids altar. Rozel harbour situated at the foot of mountainous ground is much frequented by French boats that run

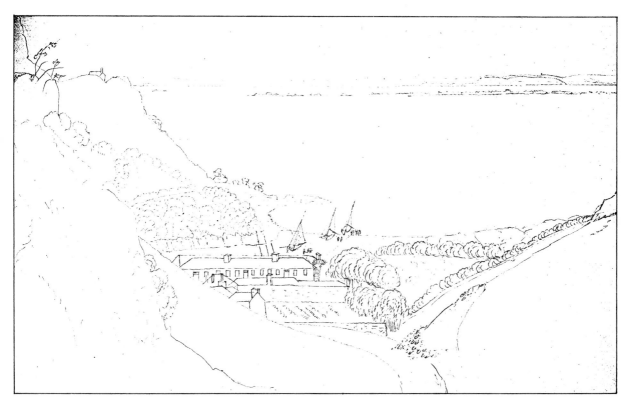

22.   Military Barracks at Roselle Bay, French boats just arrived with cattle, French distance & Rocks.

over from the opposite coast with cattle etc. It is the shortest passage to France. A boat entered whilst we remained here after a run of 4 hrs. The distance is called about 18 miles. We entered a publick house here to seek shelter and refreshment as the day was extremely sultry. When a good looking girl entered the apartment where we sat, and finding we were inclined to be sociable, she brought her tea equipage from another room and remained with us. She had just landed from the opposite coast. On her breast she wore a large brass crucifix which had been blessed by the Bishop; she told us the clergy about Barneville had received a great many of these crosses from Paris, which they had orders to distribute to the people. We took our leave of Ma'mselle and mounted the hilly eminence between us and Bouley bay. The coast of France was very distinct to our view; the cornfields and even houses were discernable. The sea was studded with innumerable rocks at ye distance of 6 or 7 miles from the land, most of which are covered at high water and are extremely dangerous in so narrow a channel, where the tides set so strong and in such various directions. Boulay bay is only one mile from Rozel harbour; it is a deep clean water and sheltered from N.W. winds. Line of battle ships may ride here at low water and it might be rendered very secure for a fleet. A deep broad mound of earth named Caesar's wall joins up to the East side of this bay and runs across the isthmus formed by it and Havre Rozel. The Romans are supposed to have had an encampment here. Sark, Alderney and the island of Guernsey were visible from this point, and a very extended line of the French coast from Cape Carteret westward. It was now nearly 4 o'clock and as we had to return to St. Helier for dinner, we thought it time to quit the coast and we directed our steps towards Delmaine the property of the late Mr. Lempriere.[7] We enquired our way and were conducted by a good looking young man up a spacious avenue thru a wooded and well cultivated estate. He informed us that the property we were on consisting of about 96 vergees of land belonged to him. His name was Prichard; the house and out-buildings were suitable for any gentleman. The grounds of the late Mr. Lempriere were close adjourning. They had a park like appearance from the quantity of wood and the arrangement of it. The property is now divided, having been sold since his death. The Gates and avenue of beech trees leading to the scite [sic] of the mansion which is now pulled down are ancient and are entirely neglected. The trees have arrived at their full growth and are uncommonly high. We reached home by St. Saviour's at ½ after 5 o'clock when we dined and at 10 o'clock retired to our chambers.

Thursday August 2nd. Our friend Captn Fischer was unable to proceed this morning having sprained his ancle [sic] the day before and as we hoped that a little rest might recover him we determined to devote this day to the charming scenes in the neighbourhood of St. Helier. It was one of the warmest days we had yet experienced, without a breeze to enliven us; we did not regret this respite from our fatigues, which were rendered excessive and much increased by the total want of accomodation in the country. We were obliged to return every night to sleep at St. Helier. We all met together at a 5 o'clock dinner and passed an agreeable evening.

Friday 3rd. We were obliged this morning to abandon the hope of Capt. Fischer accompanying us further on our tour and at ½ after 6 o'clock we set out in a very doubtful state of the weather; it was a dense fog with a light drizzling rain, but from the warmth of the atmosphere we judged it would turn out favorably before we arrived at the town of St. Aubins. However, we were almost wet through. We breakfasted here; it is four miles from St. Helier situated at the farther extreme of the bay. We were detained some time in the house, but we observed the mist rolling up the sides of the precipices and at last it was totally dispersed by the power of the sun. A beautiful day ensued. We walked round the wet dock and surveyed the town. It is situated at the foot of very steep ground, and consists of a few tolerable houses, much confined for room. We saw several good ones situated amidst the wood on the verdant slopes of the bay. The dock is of considerable size, and has lately been made very complete by the addition of another wall which affords perfect security. This new wall which is of great length and built of granite was undertaken and completed in twelve months at the expense of the States. A tax of 1/- per gallon on brandy is collected to defray the cost of erecting it. A small castle situated on the outside of the harbour commands this side of the bay, and a new wall has been built up to it which affords water at neap tides for vessels to repair and fit out. St. Aubin owns about 30 sail of ships, and employs 600 seamen chiefly in the Newfoundland trade. Between 12 and 1 o'clock we again set out ascending a deep defile which brought us to the heights overlooking St. Brelade's bay. We descended to the shore which is a firm white sand bounded by steep and rocky precipices bearing very little vegetation. The church is situated on the northern side of the bay, almost washed by the waves. It is very ancient. There are a few open boats here. We now ascended the high land in the direction of the Corbiere which forms the westermost point of the bay of St. Owen and which ships usually make in their approach to St. Helier from the westward. Here the deep and extensive bay of St. Owen showed itself on our righthand, defended by five martello towers and other works. In this bay the Prince of Nassau attempted to make a descent on the 11th May 1779. Blake also anchored his squadron in it before he effected the landing of the Parliamentary forces. We followed its shore which is sandy interspersed with rocks. Close to it is a lake called the Mora covering from 20 to 30 acres of land, and said to have produced formerly the finest carp. Some measuring as Falle the historian says 3 ft 6 inches in length. Its margin is much encumbered with weeds. On the banks we observed large quantities of the bone of the cuttle fish. We pursued the bay to its furthest extent and returned home thru the parish of St. Owen, visiting ye church which has not anything remarkable and passed thru the commodious barracks of St. Peter, capable of containing about 700 men. They are distant from the church about ¾ of a mile. The road here runs through a sweet part of the country, well wooded and leads down to the shore of the bay of St. Aubin. The westernside of the island is hilly and destitute of wood, but it is well cultivated. It bears a resemblance to the general scenery of the Isle of Man. The labourers were here busily employed in the harvest. We returned home by ye shore of St. Aubin and joined Capt. Fischer at ½ after 5 o'clock. He was impatiently expecting us with a well covered table. We found him much recovered from the effects of his accident and we passed a very agreeable evening.

Saturday 4th. This was market day and from ye appearance of the sky we judged it would be an extremely warm one. We breakfasted at ½ past 7 o'clock and afterwards accompanied Capt. F. to the market, where as Procurator he made necessary the purchases for that and the two following days. The Conger eel is here remarkable for its size and the people are remarkable for being very partial to it. We saw very large quantities of this fish exposed whole and others cut up in lengths selling at 2d. per lb. We had not acquired a taste for this fish which is much used for soup. Soles were large but scarce and dear. The plaice fluke was still more so selling at the rate of 8d. per lb. for good sized fish. We purchased a grey mullet for which we paid 6d. per lb. It is considered here a choice fish.

We now set out to continue our survey of the coast from Bouley bay passing along the high road leading through the parish of Trinity. It had become extremely hot and sultry, not a cloud sheltered us from the scorching rays of the sun. From Trinity church the land falls rapidly down to the shore of Bouley bay. Several small vessels were entering it as we approached perhaps from the opposite coast to which it lies convenient for any purpose. From the point of land called Belle Hougue which is a bold and steep promontery near Bouley bay we commanded a most extensive view of the French coast. These mountainous slopes are clad with fine verdure and afford a rich pasturage for sheep. They are extremely precipitous and what with the overcoming heat of the day and the insecure footing we found our progress to Havre Giffard and Bon nuit was extremely slow and difficult. The land on this part of the coast rises like a wall out of the sea, but it is well clothed with herbage. At Bon Nuit there are barracks for the Royal Artillery. They are small but very complete. The path led us down to the shore of this small bay where we found many boats, and as we ascended the steep height above, we noticed six others at anchor round a point of land. They were employed in fishing for Congers.

Scrambling up this height was the most overpowering part of the days work. The sun poured its meridean splendour over a glen which for its depth and narrowness became a perfect focus for its rays and we soon found ourselves in a

23. Orgueil Castle & harbour Jersey.

state of fusion. A small pothouse afforded temporary relief. Notwithstanding the excessive heat we continued our advance along the coast to Frimont and Rontez, near this point are the stone quarries of St. Johns, where beds of the purest Granite are worked. We observed blocks ready dressed destined for London. They were supposed to weigh five tons each allowing 160 lbs. to a square foot which is the calculation at the Quarry to which add 10 p.ct. for English weight. There were other pieces intended for pillars measuring 16, 18 and 20 ft. in length and generally from 2 to 2½ ft. in thickness. The quarry men had come to a block of very large dimensions without a flaw in it. This was measured and found to be 30 ft. broad in front and 20 ft. deep. They were boring a hole 13 ft. deep in order to blast it. From this quarry the new dock at St. Heliers is supplied with stone. We enquired the cost of it at the quarry and found that pieces of 2 ft. in length ready dressed were worth 1/- each, pieces of 3 ft. and about 1 ft in thickness 2/6 etc.

We continued our route along the coast as far as Sorel point, when ye lateness of the day determined us to direct our steps homewards. The church of St. John lay in our way, and at the village we were obliged to refresh ourselves. A pint of cidre qualified with two glasses of brandy cost us 5d. From St. Johns we followed the high road leading thru St. Lawrence and so down to the bay of St. Aubin.

the purest Granite are worked. we observed blocks ready dressed destined for London; they were supposed to weigh five —
tons each. allowing 160 tb to a square foot
which is the calculation at the Quarry, to
which ade 10 \$Ct for English weight —
There were other pieces intended for pillars
meas^g 16. 18 & 20 ft in length & generally
from 2 to 2½ feet in thickness. The quarry-
-men had come to a block of very large
dimensions; without a flaw in it; this
was measured & found to be 30 ft broad in
front & 20 ft deep. they were boring a hole
13 ft deep in order to blast it. From this
quarry the new dock at St Heliers is supplied with stone. we enquired the cost of
it at the quarry & found that pieces of
2 ft in length ready dressed were worth
1/ each; pieces of 3 f: & about 1 ft in thick-

We admired several good houses on this road which has nothing else to distinguish it from almost all the public roads on the island. We were precluded the possibility of obtaining any general view of the country owing to the closenes of the trees and fences until we began to descend towards the bay, when the rich blue expanse of water and the villas situated on its shores glistening with a most brilliant evening sun delighted and exhilarated the senses. We found our friend Fischer most impatiently expecting our arrival and we sat down to an excellent dinner with an appetite heightened by the pleasures of the day. A bumper of superexcellent cherry bounce crowned the evening. At 10 o'clock we extended our wearied limbs to repose.

Sunday 5th. A fine morning we breakfasted at 9 o'clock and attended Service at 10. The chapel is situated close to the beach. The Revd. Messrs Poigneau, Francis Guitau and Navet do duty and are assisted by Father Carroll. Mons. Nave is at present in France. The Catholics here are pretty numerous consisting of foreigners chiefly French. There is a mass at 8 o'clock and a second at 10. The responses are chaunted by the congregation at the last which has an odd effect. There is a sermon in French after the gospel and another is preached in English by Father Carroll after mass. A second place of worship is much wanted at St. Heliers; many are excluded from prayers for want of accomodation.

We dined at 3 o'clock and afterwards walked to see the Hougue Bie or Tour D'Auvergne situated about 3 miles from the town of St. Heliers. This tower is said to have been built by a Frenchman who possessed landed property at Coutances and who wished to have a view of it from this island. It is said he was murdered here by his own servant who afterwards espoused his widow. The place was in ruins till Gen. Gordon purchased it for the sum of £350 and put it into repair. There is about an English acre of ground belonging to it. The tower is built on an artificial mound of earth which is covered with trees and as the natural situation is also elevated it commands a view of all the island which appears like one large garden rising out of the sea. The stranger should not neglect visiting this station. The coast of France with the town of Barneville we distinctly saw. The rocks of Chaussee lying in the intermediate distance. We understood this delightful spot (the tour D'Auvergne) was again on sale, a considerable sum of money must have been laid out in repairs by the General who has now quitted the island. It is a delightful summer station. We returned to our lodgings and retired peaceably to our couches at 10 o'clock to prepare ourselves for a long day on Monday.

Monday 6th. This morning was ushered in with a heavy fogg [*sic*] and gloom, but we expected a fine day and set out on our journey at 9 o'clock with the intention of visiting Trinity manor, the seat of Captn. Carteret of the Navy. It is distant about 4½ miles from the town of St. Helier and one from the church of

Trinity. A handsome avenue planted with trees leads from the high road to the house. As we walked up we fortunately fell in with the Bailiff Mr. Pedder, who was at the plough in a field close to the road. He was extremely civil and quitted his employment to conduct us thru the grounds. This estate is the largest in the island and is all rich arable land, consisting of 200 English acres, but owing to its elevated situation it is scarcely ever free from fog, even during the summer months, and a rather sharp cold air prevails, very prejudicial to vegetation. Trees flourish and attain a fine growth, but the bark may be observed to be covered with a species of lichen from this cause.

The gardens and shrubberies were under the management of an English gardener. There was nothing to remark here, if we may except the hydrangeas which had attained an extraordinary size, and flowered strongly; one plant bearing as the gardener told us one thousand heads of flowers. The Admiral is said to have been the first to introduce this plant from China when he accompanied Lord McCartney's embassy there. The family portraits in this house are numerous and well preserved, but the steward was only permitted to show the Hall and one other room. Over the mantlepiece of this, we noticed the portrait of Admiral de Carteret, father of the present gentleman, formerly Capt. Carteret, who circumnavigated the globe. There was also a good Neapolitan Bacchante by Salvator Rosa. The Hall contained many relics of savage art which had been collected by the late possessor, such as dirks, muskets, buffalo horns etc. Mr. Pedder is a native of the Isle of Wight and appeared to us a very superior person by his manners and conversation. The estate was undergoing a complete reform under his superintendance in which the English style was visible; the grounds assuming a more park like appearance and being laid under more regular crops. He told us that Capt. Carteret had been 12 months in England and that when he returned he intended to take down the old mansion and erect another under his directions. In the front of the house he pointed to a flat stone about four feet square and raised on a pedestal 2 ft. from the ground on which King Charles is said to have partaken of many festivities during his abode in the island. The flagged court in front of the house which formerly was kept in neat order, enclosed and flanked by turrets, has been sodded over by the present proprietor and the turrets removed.

We pursued our course from here towards St. John's church, distant 4½ miles and so on thru St. Mary's to Plemont height, at the extremity of which the small remains of Castle Gronez appear; an Archway entrance only, denotes where the fabric stood. The land is high, covered with heath, and quite bare of wood. A Signal Station was pitched here during the war and now stands in ruin. Hence we followed the road leading past St. Ouens and St. Peter's churches; we were as usual almost lost in the deep wooded lanes until we approached the bay

to our couches at 10 o'clock, to prepare ourselves for a long day on monday —

Monday 6th This morning was ushered in
with a heavy fogg & gloom, but we expected a fine day, & set out on our journey
at 9 o'clock with the intention of visiting Trinity manor the seat of Captn
Carteret of the navy, it is distant about
4½ miles from the town of St Helier and
one from the church of Trinity. A handsome, road avenue planted with trees —
leads from the highroad to the house.
as we walked up, we fortunately fell in
with the Bailiff, Mr Pedder, who was
at the plough in a field close to the road
he was extremely civil & quitted his employment to conduct us thro' the grounds.
This estate is the largest in the island & is
all rich arable land, consisting of 200

of St. Aubin, towards which the land gently declined. Here, the most beautiful situations may be selected for villas. St. Peter's is a good village and the land around it lies well, commanding good views and being well clothed with wood. Near to the shore we noticed a vine covering the whole front of a house; it had a remarkable, narrow and deep indented leaf. The bunches of fruit were more numerous than the leaves. We understood it to be the white currant cluster. At ½ after 5 o'clock we arrived at St. Heliers and were glad to sit down with our friend Fischer to a good dinner, which he always provided for us, with the current news of the day. The critical state of the Queen's health, owing to a sudden inflammatory attack, had been made known this morning by the arrival of a packet and caused much sensation, her recovery being considered extremely doubtful.

Tuesday 7th. We had now completed a most laborious, but interesting tour thru the island and we had inspected all its churches, except St. Martin's which adjoins Grouville. The necessity of our returning home every evening to sleep gave us an opportunity of quartering the interior and varying our road as much as possible. We passed this day in examining the new dock particularly; it is very capacious, being nearly 700 yds in length and perhaps 50 in breadth. At the end near the entrance are two deep recesses where large ships find more water. It is a dry harbour with a good even bottom of dry clean sand; immediately above rise the town heights which within the last few years have been considerably improved, and very strongly fortified. These works most effectually command the town and neighbourhood, Elizabeth Castle and the adjacent part of the bay of St. Aubins. We went into the Regents Fort which is the mainwork on the height. Its form is that of an irregular paralellogram, extremely capacious, and furnished with bombproof casements, the ramparts afford a beautiful and extensive walk. Most of the guns, particularly those over the town, are now dismounted and the embrasures masked. It is said that the erection of this work caused an unpleasant feeling amongst the inhabitants of St. Helier, who suspected that on its completion, additional taxes would immediately be laid upon them. There are three gates to the entrance of the Regent's Fort, the centre one is formed of an iron frame, filled up with chainwork. Over the inner gate is an inscription with the date of the work, the first stone of which was laid by Gen. Don in 1812. On the South side of these heights, and below them, are engineer Barracks; they are capacious and stand on rocks, washed by the sea. This is the general bathing place.

St. Heliers posesses many good ships trading to the Brazils and Mediterranean. Three or four sailed during our stay here, and a new one belonging to Mr. Janverin was just launched and was fitting out. Sixteen privateers belonged to St. Heliers during the war and enriched many individuals concerned in them.

village, & the land around it lies well, commanding good views, & being well clothed with wood. Near to the shore we noticed a vine covering the whole front of a house; it had a re--markable narrow & deep indented leaf; the bunches of fruit were more numerous than the leaves; we under-stood it to be the white currant clus-ter — At ½ after 5 o'clock we arrived at St Heliers, & were glad to sit down with our friend Fischer to a good dinner, which he always provided for us, with the cur-rent news of the day: the critical state of the Queen's health, owing to a sud-den inflammatory attack, had been made known this morning, by the ar-rival of a packet, & caused much sen-sation, her recovery being considered

24.   Grouville Church Isle of Jersey.

None but small vessels can enter the dock before half flood, but there is shelter in the deep bay of St. Aubin, under Elizabeth Castle. We met Capt. F. at 5 o'clock and partook of an excellent dinner and a bottle of Frontigniac, and retired to rest at our usual hour.

Wednesday 8th. This morning the weather looked very unpromising and a fresh breeze blew from the Westward. The Weymouth packet, with the mail, was preparing to depart, and our friend Fischer took leave of us to return home by her to Guernsey. We settled our bill of expenses for our stay here of 13 days, which amounted to £5.11.6d. and including wine etc. averaged about 3/10d. per day for each of us; we amused ourselves in rambling about the town and its neighbourhood, and making sketches. We also ascertained what vessels were sailing to Plymouth and found the Joseph and Jane, cutter, ready to proceed the following day if the weather proved suitable. We dined on a French leg of mutton which was delicious, and drank the health of our friends in England in a bottle of very good Frontigniac. There are a variety of wines to be had here, consisting of Port, Sherry, Lisbon, Madeira, Tenerife, Mountain, sweet and dry. Frontigniac, Claret, Champagne, Burgundy, Vin de Grave, Roussillon, St. George, Picardin, Hermitage, Sicilian, and Massala, which are all low priced, except Champagne, the last sells at 6/- per bottle. The best of course are to be found at the Wine merchant's store, but the common sort are retailed in almost every shop. Cordials and liqueurs may be purchased at 2/- per bottle except Martinique, and some few others which are 3/6d. English Bank notes bear a premium of 1/6d. and an English shilling passes current for 1/1d. Bills on London are worth 7½ p.Ct. in the course of exchange.

On the town heights formerly stood a Druids Temple of considerable dimensions. The stones were removed on the ground being broken up, and are now erected in the Park of Genl. Conway in England. We saw a perfect model in wood of this Temple, in the possession of Mr. Vonberg, auctioneer and salesman. It formerly belonged to the collection of the Prince de Bouillon, whose effects were all disposed of at his death, by auction.[8]

The Pump water on this side of the island is all bad; a strong chalibeat spring is used for general purposes, which becomes turbid on its admixture with spirits. The orchards had all suffered during the severe weather in the spring. No less than 90,000 hhds. of cider were made 1818; and this year it is supposed will not produce 1,000. It is said to be of excellent quality. Fall [*sic*] states that it is equal to the best red streak.

Thursday 9th. The weather still continued unfavorable and boisterous from the N.W. There was no prospect of embarking and we employed our time as usual in visiting the different emminences, and remarkable situations about the town. This day we recd. letters from England, brought by the Packet which had arrived the evening before. They were the first private accounts, that had reached us, since our departure from home, but they left us still in a state of uncertainty, with regard to the Queen's probable demise. In consequence of a wish expressed by our friend Mr. Jas. Leigh of L'pool we proceeeded to the cattle market here, to make enquiries about the prices of three year old heifers, but as the sale was not held till the following day, we were under the necessity of deferring our enquiries. We called however upon our butcher and from his information we found that the prices do not vary from those of Guernsey. Heifers of three years old average from £10 to £12 p.head, and good milk cows sell as high as £16 to £17, which agrees with the information we received from Mr. Brock the present bailiff of Guernsey.

A cargo had been shipped off during our stay here, and our butcher expressed his surprise that they could be made to pay in England. He had reason to believe that many of the Beasts shipped from hence are imported from France. Great numbers are brought over from Carteret and are landed at Rosel. After being pastured here for a time, they may find their way to the English market as Jersey cows. There is a very handsome and convenient market for cattle just completed; it adjoins the general market and is open on every Friday

The houses in St. Helier are well built and kept in a very neat state, they are generally about two stories high. The streets are well paved and kept clean. The Theatre is no better than a barn, but there is a handsome modern structure as a Jail. Public assemblies are held in a large room in Deals Hotel, a house well frequented. There are several other hotels that afford good accomodation, the York, British, Commercial, Union etc. which make a very good appearance. There is also a public room, where Newspapers and various pamphlets may be read. Cards are allowed and in the evening you may join in a sociable game at Whist till 10 o'clock. It appears from the published accounts that upwards of 70 vessels at present belong to the port of St. Heliers, of which the largest is about 350 tons. Messrs. Janverin & Sons are the principal owners.

There are many beautiful houses and ornamented cottages in the wooded environs of St. Heliers which give an additional charm to the delightful walks in its neighbourhood. We dined at 4 o'clock and passed the evening as usual.[9]

Friday 10th. The weather this morning appeared a little more settled, but it still blew fresh from the Westward. After breakfast the Captn of the Joseph & Jane cutter, called upon us to say that he should sail at 10 o'clock; we accordingly prepared for our departure, and after taking an early dinner repaired on board. At 3 pm we set sail from St. Heliers pier. The wind was directly ahead of our course and setting against a strong ebb tide, raised a very heavy sea. We were 17 passengers in number, and most of us obliged to retire to our berths from sickness. The Cutter was only 29 tons, but she proved an excellent sailer and good sea boat.

The sea on the coasts of these islands is always in a state of agitation from the velocity and great variety of the currents, which in spring tides run at the rate of 7 or 8 knots p. hour.

At 6 pm we carried away the bobstay from the violent pitching of the vessel and we had no sooner repaired it than the same accident occurred again, and during the night we were under the necessity of heaving too twice to repair other damages. On Saturday at 4 am we were only abreast of St. Pierre, Guernsey; at 6 we had reached St. Martin's Point, when we tacked ship and steered a S.W. course along the south side of the island. About Meridian we came abreast of the Hanoir rocks[10] under Plymont. Here we again tacked ship and stood North with a fresh breeze for the English coast, which we made at 5 o'clock am on Sunday morning. Berry Head bearing N.W. distant about 5 leagues, with the coast extending Eastward, as far as Portland Isle, and Westward to the Start point. About 5 miles from Berry Head we tacked ship and stood in for the bold shore off Dartmouth harbour: at 10 o'clock we were close in with the entrance to Dartmouth harbour, and distinctly saw the town and Castle. We counted 10 sail of vessels, beating to the Westward off Start bay. The day was most beautiful, which gave a rich effect to the landscape. The country is richly cultivated to the very brink of the rocky precipices and in some parts to the waters edge. We entered Start bay and coasted along its shores in order to avoid the tide of ebb which was setting out strongly against us.

The village of Stoke Fleming with its church appeared on the West side of Dartmouth and soon after the smaller one of Tarcross near to which is seen Whitcombe, the seat of Mr. Allsworth M.P. The shores here sloped gradually to the water and are covered with a beautiful verdure. The small fishing Hamlets of Allsands and Beesands situated on the shore, had a picturesque and lively appearance; we ran close up to the latter and hove too, about a quarter of a mile from the shore. A boat came off to us having crabs to dispose of. We purchased three very large ones for 1/-. As we could not proceed till 9 p.m. we went ashore in the boat and took the Cabin boy with us to procure milk. We directed our steps towards a farm house about a quarter of a mile inland where we met with a very civil reception from the proprietor. He had extensive orchards and showed us thru his cider stores and supplied us with abundance of milk. We now found it was time to return to our vessel supplying ourselves with fine large crabs, which are taken here in the greatest abundance.

The shore of this bay is of the finest gravel and the water is deep and transparent. At 9 p.m. we made sail and got as far as the Start Point, when the wind entirely died away and we were drifted along to the Bolt Head. At 3 a.m. the breeze sprung up from the Southward, when we immediately set square and studding sails; at 6 a.m. we made the New Stone, bearing North about 2½ miles. At 7 we were abreast of it; here we observed a large fleet of fishing boats, beating out from Plymouth; at 8 o'clock we passed the East wing of the breakwater, with numerous vessels employed in sinking stones. At ½ past 8 o'clock we passed under St. Nicholas island and sailed thru the Cremil passage into Stonehouse Pool, where we came to. We landed at the Kings Stairs below Mount Wyse and took up our quarters at the Crown inn.

Monday Augt. 13th. We passed this day in viewing different parts of the town. The scenes about Dock are very imposing and so diversified that a fortnight may be passed and each day will present some new feature. In the Hamoaze some of the proudest vessels of the British navy lie secured, but this water does not appear till you ascend the summit of a hill, on which is placed a redoubt, from hence a most extended panorama view embraces the whole of Hamoaze, in which we counted from sixty to seventy sail of vessels laid up in oridinary. The

Tamar and St. Germain rivers are also seen, falling into the Hamoaze by Makere Heights, and the picturesque woods and park of Mount Edgecomb. At 5 o'clock dinner was served in a most comfortable style, and we were glad to introduce ourselves into clean and comfortable beds at an early hour.

Tuesday 14th. This morning we arose completly refreshed from the effects of our sea passage. The morning was dark and misty and it blew extremely hard from the N.W. As we had not yet procured our luggage from the Custom house which is situated at Plymouth about one mile distant, we walked to that place and fortunately met the cart returning with it. We proceeded however to the Citadel which is built on an eminence commanding Catwater and the Sound. It is well worth seeing and the views from its ramparts are highly interesting and extensive. In the centre of the Citadel is a bronze statue of Charles, and over a handsomely carved Gateway we observed the date 1675. We afterwards explored all the town and quays. A new and expensive Custom house has been erected and also an Exchange for the merchants. The evening was setting in with rain and we returned home about 3 o'clock but as it soon cleared up again, we determined after dinner to visit the Breakwater and accordingly embarked at the King's Stairs – a pleasing sail soon brought us to it and we landed at the Flag staff which had just been raised on this magnificent work. Steps had been formed for the accomodation of visitors. It was now highwater and the sea broke with tremendous force on the outer face of it, whilst within the water was un-ruffled. The form of this Breakwater is a right line with the wings inclining inwards. In the centre of it is an inward projection designed for the accommo-dation of boats, thus:

It is one mile in extent. After picking up specimens of the marble of which it is composed, we returned homewards and landed at 9 o'clock.

The Breakwater is not yet raised to its intended level, and in high spring tides and rough weather the surf breaks over it, but not so as to affect the tranquillity of the harbour within. It is intended to cement and cramp together large blocks of marble on the surface structure, now raised, so as to form a convenient and splendid promenade. A tower is to be placed on each wing, lighted with Argand lamps.

After a glass of excellent Punch for which the Crown stands unrivalled, we retired to our hammocks.

Wednesday 15th. This was the feast of the Assumption. We attended prayers at Mr. Costello's chapel, Stonehouse, late Mr. Guibert's, and afterwards proceeded to explore Mt. Edgecumbe and Maker Heights, which command the finest views of the surrounding scenery. We descended into the bay and town of Cawsand, where the Pilchard fishery is extensively carried on. The town is miserable and filthy to a degree, and the bay is hemmed in with rugged rocks. Here are not less than 70 or 80 boats employed in the Fishery, which for the last three years has been totally unproductive. We visited the curing houses. They rise on the edge of the beach and are commodious structures. The place has fallen into decay since the war but chiefly owing to the cause before mentioned. We now returned and took a boat from Cremill Passage up the Hamoaze to view the wooden walls of old England. These Bulwards float in three lines, forming as it were two streets,three miles in length. We sailed up one and down thru the other, noticing particularly in our progress the San Josef and the Brittannia, a new first rate of 130 guns. Saltash a distance of four miles from Dock bounded our excursion, beyond which place the deep and beautiful Tamar takes its course. We observed three or four vessels higher up than Saltmarsh. The river St. Germains falls into Hamoaze a little below Saltash and presents the most beautiful scenery. On its left bank we noticed and admired the beautifully wooded grounds of Mr. Carew, sloping to the waters edge and a little higher up Ince Hall, beyond which Lord St. Germains grounds, and the Keep of Trematon Castle are seen, the whole forming the most beautiful coup d'oeil imaginable. We returned along the right line of the vessels moored in this beautiful water, passing the little bay, in a recess of which is placed the elegant mansion of Lady Graves. The royal Standard of England was raised half mast on board the Impregnable and Admiral Sir Alex. Cochrane had lately shifted his flag to the Windsor Castle. We dined at ½ after 5 o'clock and in the evening took our places by coach to Bristol for the following morning.

We passed two days on our way home with our old friend Mr. Hebden at Cheltenham, and on Tuesday 21st August 1821 arrived at Manchester.

This agreeable Tour occupied us seven weeks, and was performed at an expense of £23 each. Laus Deo semper – W.G.W. 1838.

An Official Account of
the French Attack, made upon the
Town of St Heliers in the Island of
Jersey in Jany 1781 —

In the Night of the 25th Decr 1750
a fire was discovered by one of the Guard
at Trinity Watch House, between Rosel
& La Coupe; it continued to burn 8 minutes
when it was answered by a similar one
on the Coast of France, which burned near
by ¼ of an hour. These no doubt were
signals fixed by the Enemy, & their emissaries employed here, for the purpose of
communicating the state of our Coast.
As it happened no English vessels were
here to protect us. The next morning, the

An Official Account of the French Attack made upon the Town of St. Helier in the Island of Jersey in Jany 1781.

In the night of the 25th Dec. 1780 a fire was discovered by one of the Guard at Trinity Watch House, between Rosel and La Coupe, it continued to burn 8 minutes when it was answered by a similar one on the coast of France which burned nearly ¼ of an hour. These no doubt were signals fixed by the enemy and their emissaries employed here, for the purpose of communicating the state of our coast. As it happened no English vessels were here to protect us. The next morning the Troops were embarked at Granville and the command given to Baron de Rullecourt, whose intention was to land here in the night during the Christmas feasts, supposing it to be a more likely season of surprising our inhabitants in a state less capable of defence than any other. The Force entrusted to him consisted of 2,000 men with whom fortunately for us, he quitted the shore in very tempestuous weather. Many of his transports were consequently dispersed & he himself with the remainder obliged to take shelter in the Island of Chausez.

Though thus impeded and his troops reduced to 1200 men, he again sailed for Jersey on 5th Jany 1781 and by 11 o'clock in the evening had reached our shore, where on a ridge of flat rock, near St. Clement bay he directed his men to disembark. Seven hundred however only effected their landing 200 being wrecked in their vessels and the rest prevented in consequence of the tide. The first step the enemy took was to seize a small battery of four guns at which there was no centinal. This they manned and having left a Company to protect their boats, in case of retreat, proceeded immediately to the town of St. Helier where to the astonishment of the inhabitants, the Market place was filled with French troops soon after the day began to dawn without a single gun having been fired or the least alarm given from any quarter. Major Moses Corbett was in bed when his servant first acquainted him with the arrival of the French troops. When he had dressed himself he found his house surrounded and on his appearing was taken prisoner. He had nevertheless privately found means to send some information of the state of things to the 78th, 83rd. and 95th Regts. which were stationed in different parts of the island. After the Lieut. Governor was taken prisoner, he was conducted to the French General who immediately proposed to him to sign a capitulation, threatening the Town with instant destruction in case of noncompliance, at the same time falsely assuring him, upon his honour, that he had landed upwards of 4,000 men in the different bays and that the few companies he had with him, (which to favor the deceit wore different regimentals) were only Pickets of the different Corps that were coming up.

The capitulation stated that all hostilities should cease, that the Castles, Forts etc. should be delivered up to M. Le Baron de Rullecourt's Forces who would take possession of them in the name of Louis the 16th that the English troops and Militia of the Island should deposit their arms in the Court House and that the former should by the earliest opportunity be sent to England in French Bottoms with all the Honours of War, that the inhabitants should be left in the quiet possession of their estates, their priveleges and their religion remaining neutral till at the restoration of peace it was determined to which of the two Crowns the Island should belong. These were the only articles worthy our notice.

The Lt. Governor represented that being a prisoner he was in consequence deprived of all authority and that therefore his signing any terms of capitulation or pretending to give any orders, could answer no purpose. The French General notwithstanding persisted in his requisition and the Lt. Governor influenced by his menaces respecting the town, and giving too great credit to his account of the Forces he had landed, was at length prevailed with to sign the Articles and to send orders to some of the officers under his command to comply with the capitulation. He however, afterwards declared in his own justification that he had not the least expectation that his orders would be obeyed, that he was convinced his imprisonment utterly abrogated his command even if he had been disposed voluntarily to exercise it, and much more when the command exercised, was the imposition of foreign force, and he therefore considered that his acquiescence whilst it protected the Town, could not possibly surrender the Island, if those on whom its protection devolved found themselves possessed of the means to protect it.

How far Major Corbett's conduct was justifiable, or how far it merited public censure is not intended here to be discussed, we refer the reader to the sentence of the Court before whom he was arraigned.

Rullecourt having gained this point, advanced to Elizabeth Castle, which he summoned to surrender in virtue of the capitulation of the Town and Island just concluded. Capt. Aylward who commanded there, not only peremptorily refused to comply, but observed that if they persisted in advancing they must submit to the consequences, and then fired a gun to convince him that he was perfectly prepared.

Rullecourt nevertheless marched forward when a second and well directed shot was sent from the Castle by which one officer lost a leg and many privates were wounded. This determined him to halt, and to send his Aid de Camp to the Castle with a Copy of the Capitulation, and a written order from the Lieut Governor Corbett to surrender the Fortress. Capt. Mulcaster, their chief engineer, received, but paid not the least attention to these directions, replying that the Castle had nothing to fear from the French, and that it was his resolution to defend it to the last extremity. The messenger endeavoured to expostulate by representing the inutility of opposing so formidable a Force, as was already landed, particularly as 10,000 more Troops were expected from France the next morning. Capt. Mulcaster then ordered a handkerchief to be bound over his eyes and having conducted him to the top of the Castle, removed the bandage and shewed him its strength, dismissing him with this reply 'The greater your Force the greater will be your slaughter'.

Nothing could exceed the rage of the French Commander, on this refusal he was compelled again to retire to the Town on which he denounced immediate vengeance. The Lieut. Governor again interceded in its behalf and sent an absolute order to the Commander of the Castle instantly to open its gates and receive its Conquerors. Mr. Charles D'Auvergne was the person compelled, much against his inclination to deliver the order to which he returned with the following written reply.

'The English Flag flying over our heads, reminds us how gallantly this Fortress has withstood the attacks of its besiegers, and I am resolved the honor of its majesty shall never be sullied whilst I am commander here' signed

Peter Aylward

During these transactions, the British Troops stationed in the Island under the command of Major Pearson [sic], who was next in command to the captive Lt. Governor together with the militia of the Island assembled on the Heights near the Town to whom the French General sent, commanding them to conform to the capitulation, but received for answer that they acknowledged no capitulation and that if the French did not lay down their Arms, and surrender themselves prisoners in 20 minutes, they would then attack them, adding that with whatever number of Troops Rullecourt may be supported, it was, their final determination to conquer or perish.

A cessation of hostilities was then demanded by the messenger, on the part of Rullecourt, for one hour, this the English Commander refused, but upon its being further urged, agreed not to advance till half an hour had expired, at the same time sending the Adjutant of the 95th Regt. to accompany him with the reply and to demand the restoration of the Governor which being refused, the issue was left to the sword. An attack was therefore instantly made by our Troops with such impetuosity that in less than ½ an hour, the enemy were totally routed and driven from the Market Place, where they endeavoured to make a stand. The Commander exasperated at this unexpected turn of affairs, did all he could to wreak his vengeance on the captive Governor, whom he obliged to stand by his side during the whole time of the conflict, which however was quickly over; the French were broken on all sides, the Baron himself received a mortal wound of which he expired that evening and the person who seconded him in command was obliged to surrender himself and the whole party prisoners of war, while Governor Corbett escaped without a wound although he had received two balls thro his hat.

In this moment of victory, fell the gallant Major Pierson, to whom this Island is indebted, for its deliverance and whose loss was most sincerely lamented by every officer and soldier, both of the Regulars and Militia as well as by every inhabitant of the Island. He was succeeded by Capt. Campbell of the 83rd Reg. who had early in the conquest distinguished himself as an able Officer and who was every way qualified to take command upon so important an occasion.

Rullecourt may justly be considered as an adventurer who having wasted the property he possessed in his own country, had nothing left to depend upon but the chance of conquering and enjoying the spoils of another. He appeared to be from 40 to 50 years of age, was a native of Low Flanders, and related to some persons of distinction in Spain in which country he was taught the first rudiments of military knowledge. He had been 19 or 20 years in the service of France, and during the commotions in Poland served in ye Russian Army where he signalised himself in surprising and capturing a Castle of considerable strength. He was second in command when Prince of Nassau made an attempt on this Island in 1779 after which he was made Lieut Colonel of the Legion of Luxemburg and he had obtained from the grand Monarch the great Cross of St. Louis upon his embarking to attack Jersey, with the promise of being made its Governor in case his exertions were crowned with success.

He appears to have been a man of courage but fierce and violent and to have been very deficient in prudence and conduct necessary for bringing a military enterprize to a successful issue. His disposition was the most irregular, sometimes full of giddy vivacity at others sullen, morose and cruel. Of the latter we shall give the following instances, during his stay at the Isle of Chausez from the 25th Dec. to the 5th Jany following with his sword he severed the head of one of his soldiers in two for no other offence than complaining of the severity of the season, and a second having expressed his dissatisfaction with the quality of his provisions, he condemned to be placed on a rock at low water mark and then to remain till the returning tide ended his existence. His inconsistancy of conduct was conspicuous to the last, he brought with him neither Fifes, Drum nor Colours, his artillery consisting of 4 Field pieces were neither landed nor used, among his troops he had between 3 & 400 felons, whom he had taken from different prisons, and to render the whole still more ridiculous, he had accepted the services of a Turk who had offered his assistance in this expedition and whose promised reward in case of success was a seraglio of Jersey ladies. This whiskered gentleman who called himself cousin to the Emperor of Morocco, engaged much of our Islanders attention, but afforded them no very exalted idea of Eastern bravery, for no sooner had our Troops entered the Market place, than pretending to be mortally wounded he threw himself upon the ground and there continued to writhe and groan as if in his expiring moments, till perceiving the attention of our soldiers directed to another object, he leaped from the spot on which he had with so much success performed this farce, ran into the Court House and there sheltered himself from the fury of those who had determined to number him among the slain, but who observing him as they imagined already in the pains of death, suffered their resentment to give way to an indignant compassion. This hero, in the early part of the day. whilst fighting was out of the question used his persuasion with the Baron to fire the Town and put the inhabitants to the sword.

Rullecourt brought with him many papers, some of which fell into the hands of some of our Officers, but a packet containing no doubt, something very essential, burnt in the town by one of their Officers, immediately after the defeat, is much to be regretted.

The most remarkable contained an estimate of the value of the shipping, effects etc. of the Merchants of the Island which according to their calculation amounted to 2,000,000 livres, there was also a great number of signed Commissions with blanks left for the insertion of names of those whom Rullecourt might have promoted, with directions to advance to the best posts, civil and military, those who had most distinguished themselves in the service, several letters from Renier, the proprietor of Chausez that indicate him to have been a great promoter of the Expedition, also Maps and descriptions of the Island and an account of 500 livres given to an engineer who in the month of November preceeding, had taken plans and made various observations upon our fortifications, military strength and discipline. This defeat put an end to all hopes the French Ministry entertained of reducing this Island, and indeed it was a source of no small mortification to them to learn that of all the Troops they landed at that time, not one escaped. The highest commendations are due to the good conduct and bravery of the Officers and men both of the Regulars and the Militia whose zeal and exertions entitle them to the first place in their Country's esteem, nor is it more than justice to their merit, that we remark among others, who were foremost in the ranks Capt. Fraser and Lt. Robinson of the 83rd. and of our Natives, the Rev. Mr. le Couteur, Mr. Clement Hemery, Mr. Patriache, Mr. Hammond, Mr. Philip Dumaresq of St. Johns, and Mr. Pipon, particularly distinguished themselves.

The following is a list of killed and wounded

Regulars 78th Light Company 1 rank & file killed 3 do. wounded
78th Battn. Company 2 rank & file killed, 12 do. wounded
83rd Grenadiers 6 rank & file killed, 8 do. wounded
95th Regt.: 1 Officer & 2 rank & file killed, 1 Serjeant 1 rank & file wounded.

Total 1 Officer & 11 rank & file killed 1 Serjeant, 35 rank & file wounded.

N.B. Captn. Chorlton of the Royal Artillery wounded whilst a Prisoner.

hands of some of our Officers, but a packet containing no doubt, something very essential, burnt in the town, by one
of their Officers, immediately after the
defeat, is much to be regretted.

The most remarkable contained an estimate of the value of the Shipping,
Effects &c of the Merchants of the Island,
which according to their calculation,
amounted to 2,000,000 livres; there was
also a great number of signed Commissions, with blanks left, for the insertion of the names of those, whom Rullecourt might have promoted, with directions to advance to the best posts, civil
& military, those who had most distinguished themselves in the service; several
letters from Renier, the Proprietor of
Chauzey, that indicate him to have been,

Militia South West Regt. 3 rank & file wounded
St. Heliers Battn. 2 rank & file killed, 10 do. wounded
St. Laurences do. 2 rank & file killed 6 do. wounded
North West Regt. 1 rank & file wounded
East Regt. 2 Lieuts, 1 Ensign & 6 rank & file wounded

Total 4 rank & file killed, 3 officers & 26 rank & file wounded.

Names of the Officers killed & wounded.
   Major Francis Pierson 95th Regt. killed.
   Lts. Godfrey & Aubin & Ensign Poingnant, East Regt. wounded
   Mr. Thos. Lempriere, Mercht. wounded.

The Enemy is supposed to have had about 26 Officers & soldiers killed & 80 wounded.

The preservation of this and the adjoining Islands, to the Crown of Great Britain is an object of the first magnitude. They must be considered as the first foreign possessions which were ever attached to the English Government. The Inhabitants derive their origin from those hardy Warriors of the North, who after several invasions obtained the complete possession of Normandy, and by one of those revolutions, of which the daring spirit of enterprise on one side, and the want of political foresight on the other, have afforded many instances in barbarous ages, accomplished in one day the conquest of England.

Their attachment alone to this nation during more than 700 years, among the successive changes of dominion, which their Brethren of Normandy underwent and amidst the insurrections and revolutions which have taken place in every other part of the British Empire, entitle them to consideration and regard.

The majesty of the Kings of England is to them sacred and inviolable. So convinced of this affection and of their determined support of the cause of Loyalty were the Fanatics under the asurpation [sic] of Cromwell that a day of public rejoicing and thanks giving was appointed in England at the news of the capture of Jersey by a formidable Army.

This they considered as the fatal blow to expiring Loyalty. The last and present War have proved that the ardour of their zeal is unabated.

FINIS

Footnotes

1. The Bretons, on passing this island, always lower their topsails out of respect to a Saint who is said formerly to have resided on it. The ruins of a chapel are yet visible said to have been dedicated to him.

2. The Guernsey measure called a Denneril contains 4 quarts English measure.

3. It may be well here to say that the Guernsey Land measure called Vergee is 17,640 square feet, 2.46 Vergees are equal to an English acre.

4. See the printed Return at the end of this manuscript cut out of the Star Jersey Newspaper 1821.

5. There is a History of Guernsey Qto. with plates by W. Berry for an Account of it See Review in Gentlemans Magazine for Sept. 1817.

6. For particulars of this attack see the official account published, a copy of which is given at the end.

7. Mr. Lempriere of Jersey was Lt. Bailiff to the right Honble Lord Carteret Bailiff of the Island. He died of consumption at Pezenas near Langaedoc May 1790.

8. For a view of the large Druidical Temple found by Gen. Conway when he was Governor of Jersey and sent piecemeal to that Gentleman's seat Park place – see Archaelogia of Society of Antiquaries, Vo 1. 8th page 383, 385.

9. Abbey of St. Helier account of, refer to Gentleman's Magazine for January 1813 page 18.

10. The Boreas English Frigate was lost on these rocks December 5th 1807 with the greater part of her crew.

List of Subscribers

Mr. and Mrs. D. L. Adamson
Mr. Brian Ahier
Mr. and Mrs. John R. Allan
Mr. R. F. and Mrs. J. L. Allenet
Mr. B. E. R. Alexandre
Rod and Jill Amy
J. F. Arthur
Mrs. Marie-Louise Backhurst
P. M. Bailhache
Mrs. Thelma Hamon Baker
Babs Barbé
Miss G. M. Barnett
Jenny Bartlett
Mrs. B. E. Bateman
Dr. Ian C. Beavis
Mr. J. L. Benest
Mrs. Marie Bennett
Mr. M. E. Best
Mr. M. E. and Mrs. P. M. Best
Miss C. Bienvenu
Mr. Eric Blakeley
Miss Anne Blampied
Mimsie Blampied
W. L. Blampied
Mrs. Jane Blanchet
Mrs. I. Bland
Dr. and Mrs. S. E. Bodkin
E. H. Bodman
Mrs. E. M. Bois
Mr. George M. Bramall, B.Arch R.I.B.A.
Larry Bradshaw
Mr. Roger N. Brehaut
Miss Georgina Brett
Mr. and Mrs. Brigitte and Joe Hermann
Mrs. Sylvia Brouard
Frederick B. Brown
Mrs. Michelle Brown
Theo Bull
Mr. H. Charles Burr
Kathleen and John Cann
Mrs. M. Case
Mr. and Mrs. P. R. Castle
Wg. Cdr. Vernon W. Cavey
Edward Choppen, Esq, C.B.E.
Mr. B. A. Clegg
Mr. R. J. Clover
Mrs. P. Clyde-Smith
Mrs. J. M. Coleman
Reverend Canon V. J. Collas
Mr. F. H. Collins
Mr. and Mrs. Michael Collins
Mr. and Mrs. C. W. R. Cooper
Mr. Francis L. M. Corbet
Mr. Victor Coysh
Mr. A. F. B. Crawshaw
Mr. and Mrs. P. Crole
Roland De Caen
G. R. De Carteret, Esq

D. A. de Jersey
Mr. and Mrs. W. J. Denning
The Revd. and Mrs. J. Dodd
Miss Lucy Domaille
Miss Joyce Downing
Helier, Ann and Alys Dreux
Mr. R. C. Dupré
Mr. F. L. Duquemin
Mr. P. M. Du Port
Mr. Anthony K. Evered
Mr. Stuart Falla
Mr. J. D. Fallaize
Ms. Kate Fallaize
Mrs. Melanie Fallaize
Mr. W. J. Fallaize
Richard Falle
Mr. and Mrs. Andrew Fay
Mr. Ray Foster
Dr. G. H. France
Mr. R. D. Gallichan
Mrs. Gillian Garner
Dr. V. Gardiner
George W. Germain
Mr. and Mrs. R. Grant
Mr. A. L. Green
Mr. J. A. Green
Mrs. Denise Gregg
Mr. and Mrs. D. F. Hall
Mr. John F. Hall
Mrs. C. A. Harbour
Mr. Ian Hardy
C. P. M. Harris
Mr. S. A. Harris
Mr. and Mrs. G. S. Harrison
Mrs. Peter Hart
Mr. Peter Hellyer
Mr. M. A. B. Hickman
Mr. Peter J. Hill
Mrs. Sonia Hillsdon
Mr. J. A. Hilton
Mrs. Janet Russell Hole
Mr. Derek Horsfall
Yvonne Houston
Rev. Brother Laurence Hughes, F.S.C.
T. G. Hutt, M.A.
Mr. C. R. Ireson
Mr. and Mrs. James R. Irwin
Mrs. Rosemary Jagger
Senator R. R. Jeune, O.B.E.
Mr. A. G. Jones
Gabriel Jones
Mr. C. E. Kelleher
Dr. John D. Kelleher
Mrs. W. J. Kemp
Mrs. A. M. Key
Howard B. King
Mrs. M. V. Kirkman

N. d'A. Laffoley
Mrs. C. A. Lainé
Mr. John R. Lainé
Mr. Michael Lambert
Doreen M. Langlois
Mr. James H. Langlois
Mr. A. D. H. Lapidus
Sir Ronald Leach
Mr. S. P. Le Blancq
Mr. M. J. Le Boutillier
Philip and Sally Le Brocq
Mr. and Mrs. R. H. B. Le Brocq
Kaye Le Cheminant
Mr. A. L. and Mrs. M. R. Le Conte
Mr. D. O. Le Conte
Mr. Stanley Le Cornu
Mr. P. E. Le Couteur
Miss J. Le Couteur Kicke
Lady Le Gallais
Dr. Michael Le Guillou
Dr. Audrey Le Lievre
Sir Robert Le Masurier
Mr. David J. Le Maistre
Dr. Frank Le Maistre, O.B.E.
Colin Le Messurier
Mr. Richard S. Le Page
Mr. Roy Le Poidevin
Mr. Nicholas Le Poidevin
Sir Godfray Le Quesne, Q.C.
M. A. Le Quesne
Mr. G. Le Rossignol
Mr. J. A. Le Seelleur
Mr. L. C. and Mrs. E. M. L. Le Tocq
Miss M. J. Le Tocq
Mr. T. C. Le Vallee
Mr. Raoul Lemprière
Mr. David Letto
Mr. and Mrs. K. G. Lewis
Miss Selina F. Little
R. and M. L. Long
Mr. Bryan G. Lowe
Mrs. Lilian M. Lucas
Jurat Max Lucas
Mr. Gabriel J. McGovern
Mrs. Yvonne Machin
Mr. Raymond E. Maddison
Ken and Wendy Maguire
P. Maindonald
James Walter Maingay
John A. Mahey
Mrs. Valerie Mahy
Mr. Michael Mansell-Moullin
James Marr
Mrs. R. C. Martel
Mrs. Peronelle Martin
Adv. R. J. Michel
Mrs. M. N. Mimmack
Paul Mimmack
N. P. Molyneux
Mr. Ian Monins
Mr. and Mrs. J. G. Mooney
Miss Judith Moore
Mrs. P. F. Morden, M.B.E.
Jurat John Morris
Mr. H. J. Moulin
Mr. M. J. C. Murphy
P. A. Neale
Mrs. J. A. Newbald
Mr. Michael Newton

Mr. H. Nichols
Miss Stephanie Nickolls
Mrs. Adele Nicolle
Rick Nisbet
Mrs. K. Paget Tomlinson
Ms. Harlene Sanders Palmieri
Miss Muriel Rougier Parkinson
Dr. Tom W. Parsons
Mrs. Susan Payn
Mr. Ian D. Phillpot
Mr. D. A. Pinel
Mr. W. C. Pinel
Mr. and Mrs. H. F. Pinhorne
Mr. S. J. Le C. Ogier
Canon P. Raban
Mr. John W. Ramplin
Gillian Rees
Kenneth C. Renault
Mrs. M. G. Reynolds
Mr. A. Ritchie
Mr. and Mrs. J. B. Ritchie
Mr. I. Ritchie
Mr. St. John A. Robilliard
Miss Y. J. Robilliard
Deputy J. Roche
Dr. Warwick Rodwell
Mrs. F. R. G. Rountree
Mr. G. R. Rowland
Miss J. Rumball
D. J. Russell
Brian Sandeman
Mr. and Mrs. L. W. Sarre
Miss K. A. Sauvary
Anthony D. Scott Warren
Margaret L. Sellers
Mr. David Shayer
Mrs. Denys Short
Miss J. R. Simon
J. Skillett-Habin
Aidan Smith
Peter Willis Smith
Société Jersiaise
Mr. D. A. Somerville
Mr. M. W. P. Stansbury
Mr. J. G. Storry, FRHistS
Mr. and Mrs. Harry R. Stranger
Mr. and Mrs. John G. Stranger
Mr. Mike Sunier
Mrs. H. S. Surface
Mr. K. W. Syvret
Pauline Taylor
R. G. and J. A. Taylor
Joan Thomas
Mary Thompson
Mrs. Fiona Thompson
Mrs. Margaret Thomson
Mr. Vernon Tomes
Frederick Melville Towers
Jurat A. Vibert
Mrs. Joy M. Vibert
Mrs. Mary Vidamour
Mrs. E. J. Walmesley
Mr. R. F. Whidborne
Mr. and Mrs. D. J. Webb
Ronald Willesden
Revd. Dorothy Wilson
Miss E. Wood Mrs. Caroline Woods
Mr. and Mrs. S. Woods
Ian B. Yeaman